THE JEFFERSONS

A fresh look back featuring episodic insights, interviews, a peek behind-the-scenes, and photos

By Elva Diane Green
Foreword by Marla Gibbs
Afterword by By John H. McWhorter

THE JEFFERSONS
A fresh look back featuring episodic insights, interviews, a peek behind-the-scenes, and photos
By Elva Diane Green
Copyright © 2022 Elva Diane Green
No part of this book may be reproduced in any form or by any means, electronic, mechanical, digital, photocopying, or recording, except for inclusion of a review, without permission in writing from the publisher or Author.
No copyright is claimed for the photos within this book. They are used for the purposes of publicity only.

Published in the USA by:
BearManor Media
1317 Edgewater Dr #110
Orlando, FL 32804
www.bearmanormedia.com

Paperback ISBN 978-1-62933-950-4
Case ISBN 978-1-62933-951-1
BearManor Media, Orlando, Florida
Printed in the United States of America
Book design by Robbie Adkins, www.adkinsconsult.com

Cover Photo: "People look for hidden meanings. We're not duplicating 'Roots' or significant moments in history. We've always tried to keep 'The Jefferson' (sic) a family show, not too rough or nasty. The operative word is comedy. Comedy is the most demanding form of entertainment and I feel we have served the category well." - 'TV People', 'Jeffersons keep going and growing." The Southtown Star, South Holland, Illinois. (Tinley Park, Illinois) December 18, 1983, Peter Meade

Contents

Foreword iv
Introduction v
Acknowledgements vii
Chapter One: All In The Family (AITF) and Norman Lear ... 1
Chapter Two: Stirring the AITF Pot 7
Chapter Three: Jefferson's Cast Biographies 12
Chapter Four: The Spin-Off 23
Chapter Five: Well, We're Movin' On Up – Season One 26
Chapter Six: Season Two 38
Chapter Seven: Season Three 47
Chapter Eight: Season Four 55
Chapter Nine: Season Five 65
Chapter Ten: Photo Section 73
Chapter Eleven: Season Six 87
Chapter Twelve: Season Seven 95
Chapter Thirteen: Season Eight 102
Chapter Fourteen: Season Nine 110
Chapter Fifteen: Season Ten 120
Chapter Sixteen: Season Eleven 127
Chapter Seventeen: After The Show 138
Chapter Eighteen: Interviews 142
Chapter Nineteen: Behind The Scene 154
Chapter Twenty: Awards and Nominations 156
Chapter Twenty-One: Production Credits 163
Chapter Twenty-Two: Afterword By John H. McWhorter 165
Index 170

Foreword

This is Marla Gibbs and I'm sure the author Elva Green asked me to do the foreword because of my 11 seasons on The Jeffersons. I thought, what could she possibly say that hasn't been said already. When she sent me the book and I began to read it, I didn't put it down until page 122. I found her research was thorough and I discovered a lot of information that I did not know. I am sure you will find this just as interesting as I did. So, enjoy the read!

Introduction

I was given the honor of writing this book because my publisher believed I was the right person to do so. I am old enough to have memories of waiting in anticipation each week to watch *The Jeffersons*, to find out what George, played by Sherman Hemsley, would be up to this time, and his wife's, Louise, played by Isabel Sanford, reactions. George's antics were a source of merriment and their neighbor Mr. Bentley, played by Paul Benedict, was a card. Zara Cully as George's mother was the perfect "mother-in-law", sarcastic, insulting, constantly looking down her nose at her "wonderful" son's wife. Florence, played by Marla Gibbs, was a pro at cutting remarks as Florence and connected with her employer in a manner that made me wonder how in the world she kept her job.

I am also a published writer, having written my first book three years before this opportunity came along. I began this project by collecting notes and photos from a gentleman who had been working on writing this book before me. Mr. Jonathan Etter spent a great deal of time gathering information to put into book form, but found his plate was much too full to complete the project. His work was truly time saving for me and provided a perfect place to begin writing this book.

After reading and organizing the notes I was given, I began my own process of research. Using specific internet sites, I gathered information that was not to be found in the previous notes. Which means more reading. Lots and lots of reading. I then began the interviewing process. My goal was to speak with a variety of people involved in putting on *The Jeffersons*, from the people who came up with the idea, to the guests who appeared each week, to the writers and directors. This was the part I loved. I had the chance to ask the questions that could help me relate this 1970s almost all-Black sitcom to today's racial issues, such as how and why so many of these episodes were written by White people. I felt that Whites could not relate exactly as Blacks would relate. But I came to realize that a script could be written about any subject to which any person would relate, such as homelessness, gang violence or mother-in-law issues and these same scripts could include lines that would make anyone laugh. I was able to find out how certain episodes came about, especially episodes like the first transgender episode to ever appear on a TV sitcom. I was able to delve into how successful *The Jeffersons* was in dealing with society's complex social issues, sexism, prejudice, sexual disease, and morals, and still retain its capacity to give the show a comedic flavor. The writers for this show were knowledgeable as to what makes something funny.

Obviously, the scripts worked. *The Jeffersons* became one of the top ten TV sitcoms from 1975 to 1985. The show and its actors won countless awards. The guests included such well-known performers as Sammy Davis, Jr., Lillian Randolph, Reggie Jackson, Rosey Grier, Billy Dee Williams, Phyllis Diller, Joe Frazier, Charo and Ernest L. Thomas, Gary Coleman, Larry McCormick, Andrae Crouch, Albert Reed, Susan Ruttan, Larry Linville, Liz Torres, Sheryl Lee Ralph, Sister Sledge, Ivor Francis, Garrett Morris, Ted Ross, and the list goes on. Today the show can still be seen in reruns.

Many of the people involved with the production of *The Jeffersons* are gone now; however, we can bring them back to the fore of our memory through the written word. I had the honor of interviewing cast members, writers, and producers, who were willing to share their experience of working with the sitcom as you will see in the body of the book. I began with Mr. Norman Lear, who developed and produced The Jeffersons. The other individuals that I was able to contact have helped make this book not just informative, but interesting, engrossing and a fun journey as a look back down memory lane and a worth-while experience for those new to this long-running sitcom featuring African Americans movin' on up. I have also added a bit of information about some of the crew members, you know, those people who do the work behind the curtains, so to speak. Cable pullers, make-up artists, hair stylists, lighting directors, camera pulley people and so on. It is quite possible that

I may have missed somebody, and I am sorry for that. The thing I want to make clear though is that every person on a set has a contribution to that show becoming a success.

Actors want to act; it is what they do best. They want to remember their lines and they want the scene to go right. I learned that by listening to those I interviewed. They did not say "I wanted to be a huge star", well, one actor did say that. Actors are happy to have work. Writers also. They have bills like everyone else. To be able to combine what they like with getting paid is the fulfillment of their dreams.

One thing I have taken away from discussions with the writers, the cast, the guests, and the crew of *The Jeffersons* is that everyone got along. Maybe that is how they were able to receive fourteen Emmy Award nominations during their run. I have had the pleasure of re-viewing episodes of *The Jeffersons* while writing this book. In my opinion, their take on and their handling of societal issues and their ability to insert humor into each situation was masterful.

This book, though mighty close, is not an all-inclusive look at *The Jeffersons* eleven season run, rather I have endeavored to provide the reader with a fresh, informative, and entertaining reading experience, using interviews, bios, and special tidbits of exciting and little-known information. My hope is that this book gives as much pleasure in the reading as it did in the writing.

Acknowledgements

I would like to thank Norman Lear for taking the time to speak with me for this project, and Nat Segaloff for hooking me up with Mr. Lear, and Cindy, Mr. Lear's assistant, who arranged to have him available for me for exactly as long as I needed him. I would like to thank Berlinda Tolbert for agreeing to an interview with me during her stay in Los Angeles. As a member of *The Jeffersons* principal cast, Berlinda deserves special mention because in addition to sharing her experiences and thoughts with me, she also provided me with the names of some of the people who worked in the background on the making of *The Jeffersons*, people I was able to contact and from whom I was able to gain additional information. Berlinda also spoke highly of me to her friend Marla Gibbs, for which I was grateful. Thank you, Marla Gibbs, for taking my calls and for being willing to share your thoughts and your time. Paula Edelstein, another contact through Berlinda Tolbert, who was with *The Jeffersons* cast and crew from the beginning, thank you for taking the time to talk with me.

I would also like to thank the guests who granted me interviews: Steve Devorkin, Renn Woods, Ernest L. Harden, Jr., Willie Tyler and Lester, Ernest L. Thomas, Lydia Nichole, and David Lee. I was able to contact Damon Evans who graciously declined to be interviewed. Thank you, Jay Hammer for getting back to me after your wife gave you my email. Thank you to the writers who granted me time for brief interviews, Mark Rothman for your wonderful back story of the "Dog Gone" episode from 1982, Michael Baser, and Michael G. Moye (this interview was a treat I almost missed) and David Lee. Thank you, Jay Moriarty for allowing me to use quotes from your book chronicling your adventures with the writing side of *The Jeffersons*. Also, toward the end of my writing of this book,

Mr. Moriarty was kind enough to offer a few suggestions regarding photos of the cast's family members who have now achieved their own fame. Mr. Moriarty also gave me some good insight into the workings of writing and producing a television sitcom, how to list the names of the show's writers, and helped with the title of this book.

My publisher Ben Ohmart of BearManor Media has been supportive of me as a writer and has trusted me with a subject that he has been working on for quite a while. I am appreciative of the patience he has shown and of the chance he has given me, as a new author, to progress. Thank you, Ben, and your great staff.

I have discovered that I am guilty of repetition, but I must mention Jonathan Etter again as it is an absolute fact that I could not have done this half as well had it not been for Mr. Etter. He provided me with copious notes and pictures. Almost seems as though he did all the hard work. Researching articles, verifying dates, typing the unexciting parts which were essential to the telling of this story, and keeping track of the notes from Gordon "Whitey" Mitchell (thank you, Mr. Mitchell) that had been written to Mr. Ohmart years ago. We thank you also for remaining available to me for the sake of clarity.

To my daughter, Melony, thank you for your support, for helping me to stay motivated and for listening to my periodic sniveling. To my social media followers, my proofreaders, and my family members from East to West, thank you for your encouragement.

Chapter One:
All In The Family (AITF) and Norman Lear

In a 2010 note to his friend Ben Ohmart, Gordon "Whitey" Mitchell wrote, "You could argue that *The Jeffersons* started on July 27, 1922, because that's when Norman Lear started." Well, I suppose you could argue that, but to my mind the beginnings of the 1975 CBS TV sitcom consisted of a much broader involvement of circumstances. Because Norman Lear was the producer of the sitcom, I will begin with his background.

Norman Milton Lear was born in New Haven, Connecticut on July 27, 1922. He graduated from Weaver High School in Hartford, Connecticut and attended Emerson College in Boston, but dropped out in 1942 to join the United States Army. He flew 52 missions in World War II and was awarded the Air Medal with four oak leaf clusters. In his note to Ben, Mitchell stated in the seven years he worked with Lear, Lear never mentioned any of his missions and looking back Mitchell realized he never mentioned his own time in Korea.

After World War II Lear began a career in public relations as a press agent. This career choice was inspired by his Uncle Jack: His uncle was the only relative on both sides of the family who could afford to flip his nephew a quarter whenever he saw him. Uncle Jack was a press agent. Lear joined a New York publicity firm. After coming to Los Angeles in the early 50s, Lear, while working at a sales job, got into writing comedy. He began by writing a sketch for Danny Thomas. He was next hired by Dean Martin and Jerry Lewis on *The Colgate Comedy Hour*. He eventually landed the position of producer of the *The Martha Raye Show*, which aired from

1954 to 1956, and he also worked on *The Tennessee Ernie Ford Show* from 1956 to 1961.

During these years Lear had become acquainted with Bud Yorkin, who had been born Alan David Yorkin on February 22, 1926, in Washington, Pennsylvania. Yorkin and Lear began working together sometime around the early 1950s.

In 1958 Lear and Yorkin formed Tandem Productions. The company name was suggested by the idea they both had of the two of them riding a tandem (two-seater) bicycle going "up a very steep hill" starting from the very bottom, according to an interview for the Television Academy with Yorkin on December 2, 1997, conducted by Morrie Gelman.

In 1959 Lear created his first television series, a half-hour western for Revue Studios called *The Deputy*, starring Henry Fonda.

In Yorkin's Television Academy interview, he stated that the two men produced their first show together in 1960, *the TV Guide Award Show*. The show featured Robert Young, radio, film, and television actor, as host. The show would be broadcast "with roughly 40 to 45 minutes of material." The show was a comedy and showcased an all-star cast. Seven categories were picked, a ballot and an envelope placed in the *TV Guide*. The TV viewers could vote and return their ballots through the mail. During the last ten minutes of each show the seven awards were announced. Yorkin said the show was "very successful."

Yorkin and Lear went on to produce the 1962 TV special, *Henry Fonda and the Family* on CBS. The show featured such guest stars as Jack Warden, Dan Blocker, Carole Lynley, Dick Van Dyke and Lew Grant. Yorkin "loved" this show. A few years later with Yorkin as Director and Lear as producer and script writer, they premiered the movie *Divorce American Style* (1967) for which Lear was nominated for the Writers Guild of America Award for Best Written American Comedy.

In the early 1970s Lear was promoting ideas he had for another TV series. One of the show ideas he was promoting would eventually become the sitcom *All in the Family (AITF)*. Norman had become aware of a British sitcom through Yorkin who had been in England "shooting a film". The show was *Till Death Us Do Part*, about a White working-class man who is prejudiced, and his long-suffering wife. Lear wanted to rework the show for an American audience featuring subjects like those on the British show that had not been dealt with on American TV, such as anti-Semitism, infidelity, racism, and women's liberation. After a couple of starts and stops with a pilot for ABC, CBS happened to get a look at the pilot, loved it and agreed to air it.

Meanwhile, a few new writers had begun to make themselves known among the various TV sitcoms; namely, Mr. Gordon "Whitey" Mitchell, Lloyd Turner, Mr. Bernie West, Mr. Mickey Ross, and Mr. Don Nicholl.

Gordon "Whitey" Mitchell (February 22, 1932 - January 16, 2009) was born in Hackensack, New Jersey. As a young man Mitchell began his career as a bass player, and as such, he led his own groups at The Village Vanguard and The Embers. He played with various big band greats such as Benny Goodman, and he played Carnegie Hall with Gene Krupa. He played with Ella Fitzgerald, Dizzy Gillespie, and Andre Previn, and that's just to name a few. Here's a fun fact: The bass solo at the beginning of the song "Stand By Me" by Ben E. King was done by Gordon "Whitey" Mitchell. After 1965, Mitchell largely ceased playing jazz and moved to Hollywood on advice from comedian Lenny Bruce after Lenny read an article Mitchell wrote. Mitchell had decided to pursue a career as a television writer. This decision turned out to be the right choice for Mitchell. He worked on shows such as *Get Smart*, *All in the Family*, *The Jeffersons*, *Good Times*, *The Mary Tyler Moore Show*, *The Odd Couple*, *Mork and Mindy*, and several Bob Hope television specials. Mitchell first became aware of Norman Lear when Lear wrote *Divorce American Style*. Mitchell co-wrote four episodes with Lloyd Turner for *All in the Family*, "Archie and the Computer" in Season 3, "Archie is Missing" and "Archie and the Miracle" in Season 5, and "All's Fair" in Season 6. Both writers were instrumental in developing episodes for *AITF* which led to *The Jeffersons*. As a writer and producer Mitchell spent seven seasons with *The Jeffersons*, he would go on to write for *Good Times*, *Mork and Mindy*, and *Diff'rent Strokes*.

Lloyd Turner (August 14, 1924 - November 30, 1992) was born in Winnemucca, Wisconsin. In early childhood he lost one of his arms in an accident. Turner attended the California School of Arts and Crafts before going to Hollywood to pursue a career as an animator for Walt Disney Studios. Turner started out working in the animation department at Warner Bros. in the Warner Cartoon Studios during the late 1940s as an in-betweener. In-betweeners had to park on the street and punch a time clock. In his words: "You moved around from room to room, talked to people, saw what other pictures were being done, go into where they're making the backgrounds, go to the other units." Turner wanted to be a writer. Seems the writers looked like they had more fun. "I heard all this laughing going along, nothing but fun city, jam sessions, and the writers seemed to be privileged characters. One day I walked into Warren Foster and said, what do you have to do to be a writer around here? The answer I received back from Eddie Selzer was, what have you written? I said, nothing. He said, go home and write something. It hadn't occurred to me that I'd have to do that. But I did. I went home, and I got a story." http://www.michaelbarrier.com/Interviews/Turner/interview_lloyd_turner.htm

Turner collaborated with Bill Scott on numerous cartoon shorts, including *What Makes Daffy Duck* (1948). In 1949 Turner teamed up with Jay Ward to create the first animated series on television: *Crusader Rabbit*. Turner also directed and wrote for the children's puppet show *Time for Beany*. In 1959, Turner teamed with Bill Scott and Jay Ward to create the *Rocky and His Friends* animated television series and its sequel, *The Bullwinkle Show*.

He did a lot of freelance work, too, writing many of the Dell comic books of the fifties with the Warner Bros. characters, as well as any number of television sitcoms and finally for Norman Lear on live action shows like *All in the Family*. Lloyd died of cancer with his wife Darlene at his side at his home in Shady Cove, Oregon. http://www.michaelbarrier.com/Interviews/Turner/interview_lloyd_turner.htm

Bernie West (May 30, 1918 - July 29, 2010) was born Bernard Wessler in the Bronx. He began performing as a nightclub comedian in the 1940s and '50s with his partner Michael "Mickey" Ross.

West was a Broadway and film star during the 50s and 60s, working with such greats as Judy Holiday, Dean Martin, and Ray Bolger. West won a Prime-Time Emmy Award for Outstanding Writing for a Comedy Series in 1973 for *AITF* for his writing on the episode "The Bunkers and the Swingers," which aired in October 1973. West won the award together with Michael Ross and Lee Kalcheim.

Michael "Mickey" Ross (August 4, 1919 - May 26, 2009) was born in New York City. He would serve as a bomber pilot in World War II. As a performer in the 1940s and '50s, he and his partner Bernie West had a stand-up comedy act, performed at small nightclubs. When the nightclub businesses started to fade, Ross and West wrote and produced acts for singers and comics, and TV shows such as *The Garry Moore Show* and *The Martha Raye Show*. West and Ross submitted a script for *AITF* in 1971 on spec (no money in advance). Lear liked the script, and the two men became story editors on *AITF*. It took Ross and West 30 years to hit the big time. (Ross won an Emmy in 1973 for *AITF*.)

Don Nicholl (August 9, 1925 - July 5, 1980) was born in Sunderland, England. He would become a successful newspaperman in London, a screenwriter, and a producer. He and his wife came to the U.S. on a visit, fell in love with the country, and eventually moved to the U.S. in 1969. Nicholl was writing for *AITF* when Ross and West joined. He eventually named his production company Nicholl Ross West. When Nicholl died his long-time writing partner Michael Ross wrote and read the eulogy at the funeral. After his death, his wife Gee Nicholl started a scholarship for screenwriters (Don and Gee Nicholl Fellowships in Screenwriting).

Eric Monte, playwright, television writer and producer, screen writer, and book author, had also begun working with Lear during this time. He had gotten his first big break when a script he wrote was accepted by Norman Lear. Monte had been befriended by fellow actor Mike Evans in 1971. Mike Evans, who had gotten a new role on Norman Lear's sitcom, *AITF*, was impressed by Eric Monte and asked Monte to help expand his role on *AITF*. Monte wrote a script and submitted it to Lear who was impressed and who hired Monte as a writer on the show. Monte quit *AITF* in 1974 to write the movie *Cooley High*.

As the work commenced, Ross and West worked together, and Nicholl worked alone. The three would then go over each other's scripts with suggestions and lines. Each of these writers would go on to write for *The Jeffersons*.

Chapter Two:
Stirring the *AITF* Pot

Work began on the casting of *AITF*. The following actors were unanimously chosen:

Carroll O'Connor was born in Manhattan, New York City on August 2, 1924. O'Connor served in the United States Merchant Marines during World War II. He acted in theatrical productions and television sitcoms during the 1950s. The TV programs included *Gunsmoke, Bonanza, The Fugitive, The Outer Limits, I Spy, That Girl*. He also appeared in movies, including *Cleopatra, Lonely Are the Brave, Point Blank, The Devil's Brigade* and *What Did You Do in the War, Daddy?* This last movie brought him to the attention of Lear and Yorkin which led to his becoming the character, Archie Bunker.

Jean Stapleton was also born in Manhattan, New York, on January 19, 1923. She began her career performing in summer stock and on Broadway and appeared in such films as *Damn Yankees* and *Bells Are Ringing*. Through the 1960s she had many television roles including *Dr. Kildare, My Three Sons, The Patty Duke Show* and more. In 1971, Norman Lear cast Stapleton in his movie *Cold Turkey*. Lear was known for continuing to stay in touch with the actors he had enjoyed working with and so Stapleton was chosen for the part of *AITF*'s Edith Bunker.

Rob Reiner was born March 6, 1947, in the Bronx, New York. Reiner was a writer for *The Smothers Brothers* TV show and had a few small roles acting in TV sitcoms. Bud Yorkin, who knew Rob's father, Carl Reiner, had known the younger Reiner as a child and knew of his writing and acting and chose Reiner for the role of Michael (aka "Meathead") Stivic, the Bunker's son-in-law. Reiner would go on to win two Primetime Emmy Awards for Outstanding Supporting Actor in a Comedy Series, in 1974 and 1978.

Sally Struthers was born July 28, 1947, in Portland, Oregon. Struthers began acting in the late 1960s. In 1970 she appeared in the movie, *Five Easy Pieces*. She had been performing on *The Smothers Brothers* show when Lear and Yorkin considered her for the part of the Bunker's daughter, Gloria. She came in for a reading and landed the part. Struthers would go on to win two Emmy Awards for Outstanding Supporting Actress in a Comedy Series, in 1972 and 1979.

During the making of *AITF* Norman Lear had begun to consider the idea of having a Black family move into the Bunker neighborhood. The Jefferson family would be used to explore Archie's bias toward Black people in, hopefully, a humorous way. The family began to be carefully developed by Don Nicholl, Michael Ross, and Bernie West. The idea of a spin-off from *AITF* had yet to materialize.

Isabel Sanford auditioned for the part of Louise Jefferson after hearing about it. The producers had seen her as the opinionated maid in *Guess Who's Coming to Dinner* and decided to give her the part. (When Sanford saw the promos for *All in the Family*, she thought it looked "like a rotten show.") Despite that, she watched it anyway, and when she heard Archie referring to Blacks as "jungle bunnies," she and her friend Juanita fell apart laughing since Archie's bigotry was so extreme, and so ridiculous.

Lear created the character of George Jefferson with Sherman Hemsley in mind. He had seen Hemsley in the Broadway musical *Purlie* and thought Hemsley's acting and dancing a "particularly exquisite performance." Lear originally intended Hemsley to appear in the first season of the series; however, as Hemsley was starring in the musical at the time, Lear decided to postpone the character until Hemsley was available. Lear would later say that Sherman Hemsley was a "gift from the Gods."

While waiting, Lear created Henry Jefferson, George's younger brother, and replaced George with Henry. Henry was portrayed by Milton "Mel" Stewart. Stewart, born September 19, 1929, was a character actor, television director and musician. Before *AITF*, Stewart had appeared on Broadway in *Purlie Victorious*.

Prior to Mel Stewart, singer, dancer, and actor, Avon Long was originally cast to play George Jefferson's brother, Henry Jefferson, but was removed based on feedback from Carroll O'Connor (See Wikipedia). Avon Long (not necessarily known to television viewers) had quite an entertainment career. His career in movies and the stage spanned four decades, including *Cab Calloway's Jitterbug Party* (1935), and *The Green Pastures* (1957). He reprised his role of Sportin' Life in the 1951 3-LP Columbia Masterworks recording of *Porgy and Bess*, the most complete recording of the opera issued up to that time. He also co-starred with Thelma Carpenter in the 1952 revival of *Shuffle Along*, which they recorded for RCA Victor.

Long received a Tony Award nomination for Best Supporting or Featured Actor (Musical) in 1973, for the role of Dave in *Don't Play Us Cheap*, in 1972. Long recreated his stage role in a film production by Melvin Van Peebles, in 1973. He would go on to originate the role of John in *Bubbling Brown Sugar* on Broadway, also appearing in several television shows. He played the elderly Chicken George Moore in *Roots*. He had a small but memorable role in *Trading Places* (1983) - he was Ezra, the man to whom Ralph Bellamy gives a miserably small Christmas bonus ("Maybe I'll go to the movies - by myself."). He died February 15, 1984.

Once Mel Stewart was hired as Henry, he was introduced into *AITF* as George's brother in "The First and Last Supper, April 6, 1971, as was Sanford. (When Archie was introduced to Louise, he asked her how she liked the *Julia* show the day before; by way of reply, she asked him how he liked *The Doris Day Show*.)

Mike Evans, the first actor to portray Lionel, the Jefferson's son, was approached by a CBS talent agent while standing on Melrose Avenue in Hollywood on his way to a class at Los Angeles City College. The agent inquired if Evans would like to read for a part in a television series. Instead of going to class that day, Evans went along and read for the part. A few days later he received a call telling him someone else had been chosen. A week after that Lear's office called, told him to come in and read for director John Rich - he got that part in *AITF*. He was introduced in the March 2, 1971, episode "Lionel Moves In."

Hemsley, as George, was introduced into *AITF* in "Henry's Farewell," October 20, 1973, when Henry leaves to start his own cleaning business. (George was made a dry-cleaning shop owner to create an excuse for Lionel to regularly stop by the Bunkers to make deliveries.) Hemsley and Stewart share their only scene together in its final minutes. The episode marked the final appearance of Henry.

Zara Cully was an actress with a long list of acting credentials She appeared in such early TV shows as *Playhouse 90* (1956-1960). Cully played leading parts in *Camille, Lion and the Mouse,* and *Oedipus Rex*. Her movie roles included *The Learning Tree* and *The Liberation of L.B. Jones* (1970), a starring role in *Brother John* (1971), and the Blaxploitation films *Sugar Hill* (1974) and *Darktown Strutters* (1975). Cully was also a guest on *Run for Your Life, Cowboy in Africa, Name of the Game, Mod Squad,* and *Night Court.* Cully's first appearance as Mother Jefferson was in the *AITF* episode "Lionel's Engagement," February 9, 1974.

Lynne Moody, who had enjoyed an extensive acting career beginning in the early 1970s, played Jenny Willis, Lionel's girlfriend, and was also added in the *AITF* episode "Lionel's Engagement." Moody originated the part of Jenny, but by the time *The Jeffersons* aired, the part had been filled by Berlinda Tolbert. The Jefferson family developed during the 1974-75 season of *AITF*, the characters becoming ever more prominent during that season.

In 1975 when NBC was looking for another vehicle that portrayed an all-Black cast, Lear was ready. In 1974 Lear had received a visit from a local Black activist group. He says "The Black Panthers came to him because of *Good Times*, one of his situation comedies at the time about an all-Black family. The Black Panthers were a local Black activist group and during this visit they questioned his portrayal of African Americans in *Good Times* as "downtrodden, always broke people who couldn't get out of the ghetto." As Lear had already formed the basis for a new sitcom about a Black family in his head and after the Black Panthers visit, he was inspired to make that Black family affluent and successful. That family would be *The Jeffersons*.

He would take the Jeffersons, George, Louise, and Lionel from *AITF* and star them in a new sitcom about how they moved from Queens to the "Eastside". In a 2019 telephone interview with me, in response to one of my questions regarding him being able to produce sitcoms about all-Black families, Lear stated "that as a Jew he grew up understanding the foolishness of the human condition, how people treated and were treated by each other." He said "he wanted to portray the truth about life in general, and that he also wanted to produce a show to depict humor in every day Black life." The idea of the Jeffersons doing better economically than the Bunkers delighted Lear and *AITF* fans. Also, it fit right in with the viewers wanting to see Blacks prospering. So, in Lear's words "we moved on up."

On January 11, 1975, *All in the Family* aired "The Jeffersons Move Up," which is seen as the pilot for *The Jeffersons*. The viewers are introduced to *The Jeffersons* cast members at that time: Mike Evans as Lionel, Isabel Sanford, as Louise, Sherman Hemsley as George, Zara Cully as Mother Jefferson, Paul Benedict as Mr. Bentley, Berlinda Tolbert as Jenny, Roxie Roker as Helen Willis, Franklin Cover as Tom Willis, and Ned Wertimer as Ralph, the Doorman.

It was while Hemsley was doing the last two episodes of *AITF* when the realization he'd be starring in a show of his own hit him: "Carroll had to sort of pull me together because I couldn't remember anything. My mind was bewildered and soggy." Carroll helped out a lot and said things like, 'Look, just relax. You're doing great and you're going out on your own now.' And Jean (Stapleton) and Sally (Struthers) also helped a lot. I really appreciated it because I was sort of panicky." *Bibliography Citation: Sherman Hemsley Interview, by Karen Herman on August 17, 2003, for The Interviews: An Oral History of Television.*

Chapter Three:
Jefferson's Cast Biographies

Isabel Sanford:

Sanford was born October 29, 1917, in Harlem, her father was a chauffeur from North Carolina, and her mother was a domestic from Washington, D.C. Her parents divorced when she was three. She attended Textile High School, and Evander Childs High School. Sanford began her acting career in public school, in many commencements and class plays first in elementary plays and then moved to high school plays. After graduating from high school, she joined the American Negro Theater and trained with Sidney Poitier and Harry Belafonte.

Sanford married William Edward Richmond in 1945 and had three children very quickly. She was divorced after five years of marriage. She would become a grandmother five times. She left the American Negro Theater to have her first child. Following the birth, she joined The Star Players, that group was disbanded when WWII came about. She took time off from acting to have her second child, but soon returned to acting to help with a drama project run by the New York YWCA. During that time, she worked with such up-and-coming stars as Cicely Tyson.

While working as a keypunch operator during the day, and performing at the YWCA at night, she was offered several off-Broadway roles in such plays as *Shakespeare in Harlem*, and *The Egg and I*. Sanford expected to work with the YWCA just a few days, but the assignment turned into years. Through the years Sanford performed in numerous roles before being cast on *AITF*.

After moving to Hollywood where she looked for film work, Sanford appeared in such plays as *Purlie Victorious*, and *The Blacks*.

The last was taken to New York where she made her Broadway debut. Her Los Angeles acting credits included productions with the Ebony Theatre where, in 1967 Sanford, and Juanita Moore appeared in the comedies, *A Day of Absence* and *Happy Ending*. The Ebony was a non-profit Negro stage company operated for 17 years by Nick and Edna Stewart as a community showcase. The Ebony was the oldest Negro stage company in Los Angeles.

Sanford was also a semi-regular for about two years on *Carol Burnett* (1968), also guest starred on *The Mod Squad* and appeared in the 1972 movie *The New Centurions*.

Sanford played the family maid, Tillie, in the movie *Guess Who's Coming to Dinner*, with Spencer Tracy, Sidney Poitier and Katharine Hepburn in 1968. On Friday, March 8, 1968, in her review of "*Guess Who's Coming to Dinner*," Dee Downey says that Sanford "perfectly handled" her "lesser" role of the family maid.

Norman Lear had seen Sanford on *The Carol Burnett Show* and cast her as Louise Jefferson in her first appearance in *AITF*. Sanford was surprised when her agent called her and told her she'd been hired for one episode. But Lear and company liked Sanford so much the next season her part became that of Lionel's mother.

Sherman Hemsley

Hemsley was born February 1, 1938, in Philadelphia, Pennsylvania and raised by a single mother who worked in a factory. Hemsley got hooked on acting when he played Fire in his first-grade fire-prevention show. For the part, Hemsley was costumed as a flame, "had a great death scene when the other kids threw water on him." Although he felt good about the applause he received when he appeared in a school play about fire safety, he didn't pursue the idea of acting since acting wasn't the sort of thing one did in such a rough neighborhood as Hemsley's. Hemsley ran with gangs but dropped out when the gang deserted him during a fight broken up by the police. Hemsley was 5ft 6 in, and weighed in at 150 lbs. He dropped out of high school, went into the Air Force, and was there for four years.

In the mid-50s, Hemsley enrolled in South Philadelphia's Bok Vocational Technical School. He originally planned to be a tailor but changed his mind when he saw how difficult it was to do the little stitches and he switched to retail sales – he hated that, then moved to restaurant training as he could eat the food. During that time, studied acting, and looked for acting jobs. Hemsley did children's plays, a local TV comedy series in Philadelphia and was a member of the famous Negro Ensemble Company and finally took a job in the U. S. Post Office for six years.

He transferred to a U.S. Post Office branch in New York in 1967, but he and the mailroom parted company a year later. "I left because I hated the post office," he said. "It was a grind; also, the job was dull. So, I just decided to quit one day and go for broke." *Interview 2003 Karen Herman Television Academy Bibliography Citation: Sherman Hemsley Interview, by Karen Herman on August 17, 2003, for The Interviews: An Oral History of Television.*

Hemsley joined Theatre XIV, where he played Gitlow in *Purlie Victorious*. After Purlie ended, he joined the Toronto, then San Francisco production of *Don't Bother Me, I Can't Cope*. Hemsley made his off-Broadway debut in 1968, in *The People vs. Ranchman*. He began acting with The Philadelphia Academy of Dramatic Arts. He made his Broadway debut in 1970 in *Purlie*, the musical version of *Purlie Victorious*, as Gitlow.

Hemsley performed in *Purlie* for three years before he got a call from *AITF*. He read with Carroll O'Conner. His direction was to be pompous and feisty. He had the thought "Oh no should I run?" The cast was professional and helped him get through it." - *Interview 2003 Karen Herman Television Academy Bibliography Citation: Sherman Hemsley Interview, by Karen Herman on August 17, 2003, for The Interviews: An Oral History of Television.*

Roxie Roker

Roker was born in Miami, Florida, August 28, 1929. She was named after her grandmother. Roker was an only child. Albert Roker, her father, came from the Bahamas and worked as a short-order cook on the beach. Roker's mother Bessie hailed from Georgia. When she and her husband and child moved to New York, she soon found a high-paying job doing domestic work for a wealthy family. Her father also worked as a porter in an apartment house, during which time he took correspondence courses. Soon he was working as the head shipping clerk for a medical supply company.

Roker wanted to act since childhood. She did well in school, appeared in children's plays, recited small pieces in church, also had music and dancing lessons - these did not sit well with some of their neighbors. Roker was not happy about how her neighbors felt: "I don't like that putdown, that when you're trying to achieve, you're trying to be white. That makes me mad. I think many times we do a number on ourselves. Black people are achievers; we're survivors." In 1942, Roker's father took her to Broadway to see Todd Duncan, an African American Opera singer in *Porgy and Bess*, later they saw Paul Robeson in *Othello*.

Roker went to Howard University because of its drama department. At Howard University where she earned her bachelor's degree in drama, she also received a minor in education. Roker's theater work at Howard was so impressive, she was awarded a six-week Hattie M. Strong Foundation Fellowship scholarship to study Elizabethan drama at the Shakespeare Institute at Stratford-on-Avon in England.

At night she appeared in various Broadway and off-Broadway productions. She was with NBC for 12 years. Reflecting on that time, Roker felt she stayed at NBC "far too long because she felt her job gave her security." During that time, she became Maya Angelou's understudy as the "White Queen" in *The Blacks* and stayed at NBC even after she had made a strong reputation for herself as an actress in the part.

It was while working at NBC that she met Sy Kravitz. Kravitz was a prominent NBC-TV news producer, and jazz promoter. He was of Russian, Jewish descent. Roker was involved with the civil rights movement at the time and dreamed of marrying a man like Martin Luther King, Jr. who was doing something for Blacks. Kravitz, white, Jewish, and divorced, with two young daughters was not exactly that man. They had a long friendship, and then they became even closer through their shared interests. His first proposal met with a "You've got to be kidding." Roker was concerned about losing her identity if she married Kravitz. Eventually the two fell in love.

Roker and Kravitz were married in 1962. Their son Lenny Albert Kravitz was born May 26, 1964. When he was six, his mother's pots and pans became Lenny's "drums." (The writer Gordon Mitchell talked about a memory he had of having dinner with Roxie and Sy Kravitz and them having to tell 10-year-old Leonard to turn down, or throw out, his guitar.)

Roker continued to work at NBC and act on the side until Lenny was five. In 1967-68, Roker appeared on WNEW-TV in NYC as co-hostess of *Inside Bedford-Stuyvesant*, the first TV program to emanate from the black community in that area.

Roker joined the prestigious New York-based Negro Ensemble Company in 1970. She was soon cast in the company's production of the Joseph A. Walker prize-winning play, *The River Niger*.

Playing the role of the mother in *The River Niger* not only won her an Obie and a Tony Award nomination, but she also won the attention of Norman Lear. She auditioned for the casting directors, then the producers. Lear and company wanted a tall, elegant East Side lady because the character was supposed to look down on George. It was not until her final interview with Lear that the producer learned she was married to a White man after asking her if she would have any problem with kissing a White man on television. According to Lear, Roker said "Let me tell it to you this way, I'm married to a white man."

Franklin Cover

Franklin Cover was born November 20, 1928, in Cleveland, Ohio. He was a graduate of Denison University, 1951. At Denison, he was active in the Denison Summer Theater in the blue tent where Burke Hall now stands.

Cover began his acting career at age sixteen. He performed on stage in the U.S., Europe, Japan, and Korea. His many television appearances included, The *Jackie Gleason Show, Armstrong Circle Theater, Who's the Boss, Mad About You,* and *ER*. He appeared on Broadway and off-Broadway in *Applause, Forty Carats, Any Wednesday, Calculated Risk,* and *Hamlet*. Cover played Macbeth during a state dinner given during the Kennedy administration. He starred in *The Man Who Came to Dinner* at the Ace Morgan Theater. He appeared in *Henry IV* at the Phoenix Theater in New York, and he appeared in *The Great Gatsby* in 1974 and *The Stepford Wives* in 1975.

Cover was financially strapped when producer Norman Lear offered him the role of Tom Willis. He was cast as a Caucasian married to a beautiful Black woman. "I took the part because I knew Norman's shows are always interesting," Cover recalled. "It was also a challenge to be part of TV's first interracial marriage." "I jumped on the plane without a moment's hesitation," he added. "I was broke, between shows and there were school fees and rent to pay."

Zara Cully

Zara Frances Cully Brown was born on January 26, 1892. Cully was a writer, singer, director, solo recitalist, and actress. She was a native of Worcester, Massachusetts, and graduated from the Worcester School of Speech and Drama. After marrying in 1914 Cully had two children.

In 1940, after an appearance in New York City, she became known as "one of the world's greatest elocutionists." After moving to Jacksonville, Florida, she became known as the Dean of Drama of Florida, thanks to the plays she wrote, directed, and produced. For 15 years she was a drama teacher at her own studio as well as at Edward Waters College. Cully became upset by the racism she experienced during that time in the South, and she decided to move to Hollywood where she became a regular performer at the Ebony Showcase Theatre.

Her first appearance as Mother Jefferson on *The Jeffersons* was January 18, 1975. She was 82 years old.

Marla Gibbs

The middle of three sisters, Gibbs was born Margaret Bradley on June 14, 1931, at Cook County Hospital in Chicago, Illinois to Ophelia Birdie (née Kemp) and Douglas Bradley. Gibbs' father was a mechanic who ran an ice business in his spare time. The family lived in a home originally owned by Al Capone's boss: 'Big Jim' Colosimo. Gibbs went to boarding school, Catholic school, and public school. She attended Wendell Phillips Academy High School in the Bronzeville neighborhood on Chicago's South Side.

She graduated in 1949. Shortly after high school, Gibbs moved to Detroit, Michigan, where she attended Peters Business School. She was married to her high school sweetheart Jordan Gibbs from 1955 to 1973 and they had three children.

Gibbs began her career on local television in Detroit in the mid to late '60s. In Detroit, she appeared on a series called *Juvenile Court*, playing the mother of a boy who had thrown a brick at a passing train and caused an injury. Gibbs received letters from viewers who believed she was the boy's mother in real life. Gibbs began acting in the early 1970s Blaxploitation films, *Sweet Jesus, Preacher Man* and *Black Belt Jones*, while working as a Reservations Agent for United Airlines. Her agent was instrumental in getting her an interview with casting for *The Jeffersons*. When she auditioned for the part with the producers, Gibbs thought of her grandmother and her aunt and read the part as if she was one of those women. By the time she got home she got the call that she had the part.

Mike Evans

Michael Jonas Evans (Mike Evans) was born in Salisbury, North Carolina on November 3, 1949. Evans was a product of a mixed marriage, his mother, Annie Sue Evans, who was White, taught elementary school in Watts, and his father, Theodore Evans Sr., a Black man, was a dentist. Evans attended Palmer Memorial Institute, a private school for young Black Americans in Sedalia, North Carolina just outside Greensboro. His family later moved to Los Angeles, where he graduated from Los Angeles High School. At eighteen, Evans went out on his own, living like a hippie. He sold the *L.A. Free Press* on Sunset Boulevard for $15 a week. Evans has said, "It paid the rent."

After landing the part of Lionel, in *AITF*, Lear chose him to continue in the same role in *The Jeffersons*.

Berlinda Tolbert

Tolbert was born in Charlotte, North Carolina. She attended Second Ward High School. As a young girl Tolbert had a stuttering problem. In her words: "I stuttered and stammered each time I opened my mouth to talk, and because of it, I felt ugly. I was withdrawn, painfully shy and 'different' in the other kids' eyes." Relatives tried to get Tolbert to talk. But when she did, Tolbert would lose her train of thought, and become overly self-conscious in a stuttering attack. The problem was so bad Tolbert got to a point where she didn't want to say a thing. But when Tolbert went to middle school, things started to turn around after she met a speech teacher. The speech teacher told her acting in school plays would be a form of therapy; Tolbert found that she enjoyed it. As a result, she developed self-confidence, and started looking at things in a positive way. "I won't allow anyone to say the words 'can't' and 'never' around the activity in my life. For me, it's 'I can and I will!'"

Tolbert majored in theater and received her Bachelor of Fine Arts degree in dramatic arts at the North Carolina School of the Arts in Winston-Salem. She toured with the Carolina Repertory Company where her first professional role was in the Carolina Repertory Company's production of *The Wonderful O* in Chapel Hill, NC. She also studied drama in London. Tolbert worked with the Negro Ensemble Company (NEC), where she met Ruby Dee and James Earl Jones, her idols. She then joined the Washington D.C. Theater Club, and appeared in *The Boor*, then at the Ford Theater, she appeared in the musical *Godspell* first performed in Washington, also when the production moved to New York. Later Tolbert worked at New York's Lincoln Center for the Performing Arts in the Joseph Papp/Woody King production, *What the Wine Cellars Buy*. During 1974, Tolbert guest-starred on various television sitcoms including the PBS show *Shoot Anything with Hair That Moves*. She also appeared on *The Streets of San Francisco*, *Sanford and Son*, and *That's My Mama* before being cast as Jenny Willis on *AITF.* Tolbert was shopping when, after checking her answering service, she found she had an urgent message to call her agent. The agent had lined her up for an audition. She had ten minutes to get there. She had on no makeup, a floppy hat, and an old pair of jeans; however, despite her unkempt appearance, she got the part. (**See Interview with Berlinda Tolbert - Chapter Eighteen**)

Paul Benedict

Paul Benedict was born in Silver City, N.M., September 17, 1938, and grew up in Boston. Benedict's real surname was Debenedetto. His father changed the name to Benedict when he came to the United States. Benedict was the youngest of six children that included three sisters and two brothers. Benedict told *TV Guide* in 1978, "When I was 4 years old, I knew without any doubt that I wanted to act." Due to his shyness, he did not begin acting until high school. When he went to Suffolk University in Boston, he planned to be a writer.

In his first job following college, he made fifteen dollars a week. He worked backstage, the box office, and handled press releases for the Charles Playhouse. A friend opened a coffee house featuring jazz and poetry and asked Benedict to manage it. A second friend had a theater group, so the three of them combined the coffee house and the theater group to form the Image Theater. This project lasted three years, with Benedict pulling in $25 a week. When that went under, he went to work at the Boston Community Theater. For six seasons he worked with Robert DeNiro, Al Pacino, Dustin Hoffman, Blythe Danner, and Robert Duvall. Benedict also did much regional theater and movies including *Jeremiah Johnson*, *Up the Sandbox*, and *The Front Page*.

Benedict moved to New York to audition for Alan Arkin in *Little Murder*, a 1969 stage play. When Benedict finished reading, Arkin told him he had the part. After Norman Lear saw Benedict in the show, he cast him in his movie, *Cold Turkey* in 1971. After *Cold Turkey*, Lear chose Benedict to play Mr. Bentley.

Ernest Harden, Jr.

Harden was born on November 25, 1952, in Detroit, Michigan. Through the family values he learned from his parents, knowing early on what he wanted out of life and staying focused, he was able to progress in the field of entertainment. He did commercials, then he appeared in *Three Days of the Condor* (1975). In 1977 he was chosen for two roles in *The Jeffersons*. His first role was as Jason King, in a 1977 episode in Season Three and then as Marcus Garvey Henderson in Seasons Four, Five and Six (1977-1979). Harden would go on to star with Bette Davis in the movie *White Mama* (1980).
(See Interview with Ernest Harden, Jr. - Chapter Eighteen)

Damon Evans

Evans was born on November 24, 1949, in Baltimore, Maryland. Evans was a voice major at the Manhattan School of Music in New York. He began his studies at Peabody Conservatory in Baltimore. He also studied singing at the Boston Conservatory of Music. He took acting lessons but concentrated primarily on music, that was where he hoped to have his career. While studying at the Boston Conservatory, Evans was cast in the Boston company of *Hair*. After that came New York, and a short-lived, off-Broadway show, which was soon followed by his Broadway debut in 1971 in *The Me Nobody Knows*, which allowed him to sing. Evans was offered the part of Lionel in 1975. He had second thoughts because of his love of singing but would accept the role, appearing in Seasons Two through Four.

Jay Hammer

Jay Hammer was born November 16, 1944, in San Francisco, California. Hammer was known for such TV shows as *Guiding Light*, *Emergency!* and *Kojak*. He also appeared in the television movie *The Mark of Zorro*. In 1978 Hammer was chosen to play the role of Tom and Helen's son, Allan Willis. **(See Interview with Jay Hammer - Chapter Eighteen)**

Ned Wertimer

Wertimer was born on October 27, 1923, in Buffalo, New York. Wertimer served as a Navy pilot in World War II. He received a Bachelor of Business Administration degree from University of Pennsylvania's Wharton School. While at the school, he became a member of the Mask and Wig Club, an all-male comedy and musical troupe. Wertimer would perform in a musical by Robert E. Dolan and Johnny Mercer, also in *The Live Wire* by Garson Kanin, *The Disenchanted*, with Jason Robards, and *All in Good Time* by Bill Naughton. He began to appear on television on programs such as *The Shari Lewis Show*. He also portrayed a detective with the Harrington Detective Agency in the "Kingfish's Secretary" episode of *Amos 'n Andy* on July 5, 1951. Edward "Ed" Wertimer was introduced as Ralph, the Doorman in the *AITF* episode "The Jeffersons

Move On Up," in 1975. His character was carried over to *The Jeffersons* as the doorman who always sought a gratuity for his services.

Danny Wells

Wells was born Jack Westleman in Montreal, Canada on April 7, 1941. His acting career spanned more than four decades, beginning in 1972 on the comedy television show, *Love, American Style*. He appeared also on, *Sanford and Son, Columbo, Ironside, Rhoda, Harry O*, and the *Shaft* 1974 television series. Beginning April 1975, Wells began his recurring role as Charlie, the bartender in the "Jenny's Low" episode of *The Jeffersons*.

Ebonie Smith

Ebonie Smith was born Negra Candalaria on September 16, 1978, in Puerto Rico. As a child actor she was chosen to play Jessica Jefferson, George and Louise's granddaughter.

Chapter Four:
The Spin-Off

Don Nicholl was against the idea of 'crossovers', he believed they should keep the Jeffersons separate from the Bunkers once the move was made. Nicholl's response to those who wondered how he could produce two shows (*AITF* and *The Jeffersons*) back-to-back: "With my left foot I crack walnuts." Paul Henniger, *L.A. Times Syndicate.*

In an interview as a semi-regular on *AITF*, Isabel Sanford was opposed to the idea of spinning off *The Jeffersons* as a separate series: "*All in the Family* was a hit and I wanted to stick with it. I'm a Virgo so I'm practical. I didn't want to go off and do something new. They said I'd be a star. Big deal. I'd rather work." When Norman Lear told Sanford there'd be a Louise in *The Jeffersons*, but not in *AITF*, she agreed to do the spinoff series. *Journal-Inquirer*, Manchester, Connecticut.

Some wondered how a Black TV show could be written about by White writers. This is a quote from an article in the *Oxnard Press Courier*, 1975: All three of Jeffersons' producers (Don Nicholl, Michael Ross, Bernie West) were White. The trio felt they could write a show about Blacks and the Black condition. They felt that all that was necessary was humanity - that they could produce a show dealing with people. What color skin those people were was irrelevant, thought the trio. Their philosophy: "it doesn't matter what color you are as long as you understand your characters and how they think and feel." Mickey Ross: "If you can write about the human condition, it doesn't matter if you are Black or White."

The program was first entitled *Those Jeffersons*. Lear chose *The Jeffersons*. It was decided that *The Jeffersons* would be a sitcom about a Black family who moves from the poor part of town into an apartment in Manhattan. George Jefferson, played by Sherman Hemsley, has opened his third cleaning establishment, Louise Jefferson, his wife (who had once been a maid), and George's mother, Mother Jefferson played by Zara Cully, who stops by now and then. The son, Lionel, is engaged to Jenny, played by Berlinda Tolbert, Tom and Helen's daughter. Tom and Helen, played by Franklin Cover and Roxie Roker were the upstairs neighbors. The fact that Tom was White, and Helen was Black would be used to provide George (a bigot) with some fuel. This was a ground-breaking point for the sitcom and TV world. Tom and Helen would be the first Black and White married couple on television. There was some opposition to this, mostly from the Deep South. There was also a British neighbor, Harry Bentley, played by Paul Benedict. It was also decided that as the Jeffersons had moved up in the world, they ought to have a maid. Marla Gibbs was chosen to play the part of the Jefferson's maid, Florence Johnston.

George and Louise's backstory begins in 1951 when they started dating as teenagers. The two got married and began married life at 126 Lennox Avenue in New York. Their son, Lionel, was born in 1953. Over time they moved to Queens. By 1968 George had been working in a cleaning establishment for five years. He worked the press machine, tagged clothes, and waited on customers. George decided it was time for him to get a piece of the pie. He applied for a loan and began looking for a place where he could open his own cleaners. While showing Louise the room where he wants to set up his store, a brick is thrown through the store window. When George confronts the people in front of the store, he learns that Martin Luther King, Jr. has been shot and people have started rioting. His outrage is immediate. He and Louise cannot believe what they have heard.

They are at home when the loan adviser comes to let them know they can have the loan, but on one condition – that they choose a better neighborhood for his establishment because of the rioters. George takes offense and refuses the loan and tells Louise that he had found his dignity. Lionel is ready to go out and join the rioters and George wants to go with him. Louise manages to calm them both by reminding them of Martin's message of non-violence. The show ends with the voice of Dr. King coming from the radio giving his "I've Been to the Mountaintop" speech: "We've got some difficult days ahead, but it really doesn't matter with me now, because I've been to the mountaintop...."

Sometime later George is in a traffic accident and receives a $5,000 whiplash settlement from the City of New York. He uses this money to start his cleaning business. George's business flourishes and he and Weezy, George's nickname for Louise, can move on up to the East Side. They move into the hi-rise Whittendale Building at 185 East 85th Street, on the 12th floor, Apartment 12D, as George opens his third store on the first floor of the building.

The theme song for *The Jeffersons*, "Movin' On Up" came about very simply. According to an article in the *TV Guide* in 1975, Janet DuBois told her boss she was pleased with her success in *Good Times* but was "aching to branch out," to show off her other skills. Lear suggested she work on the theme song to his upcoming series *The Jeffersons*. DuBois says, "I sat up that night and wrote it and had it to him the next morning. I know all about Black folks movin' up. I been there." Dubois also had a co-writer, Jeff Barry. It is DuBois who sings the song.

Chapter Five:
Well, We're Movin' On Up – Season One

Created by:
Don Nicholl
Bernie West
Michael Ross

Developed by:
Norman Lear

Main Cast:
Isabel Sanford
Sherman Hemsley
Marla Gibbs
Mike Evans (Seasons One, Five, Six, Seven, Nine and Ten)
Damon Evans (Seasons Two, Three and Four)
Roxie Roker
Franklin Cover
Zara Cully (Seasons One, Two, Three and Four)
Berlinda Tolbert
Ernest Harden, Jr. (Seasons Three, Four, Five and Six)
Jay Hammer (Season Five)
Paul Benedict
Ned Wertimer (recurring)
Danny Wells (recurring)

Studio audiences usually consist of about 300 people. They are treated to a warm-up before the taping of the show. Warm-ups are unpolished, unrehearsed, silly, and fun, the purpose is to get the audience in the mood to enjoy what they are about to see. They are usually unfamiliar with production techniques, do not know what the TV companies expect of them, and may be out of sorts over the amount of time they had to wait to get in the studio. The job of the TV people was to get the audience to relax and feel at ease. Studio audiences are especially important to the sitcoms. Bernie West, the show's warm-up host, says: "If there's a delay (in the proceedings), you try to keep them happy and interested and alert. Otherwise, they tend to get sleepy and groggy—and unfriendly." Biddeford-Saco Journal

Time Slot: January 1975 - August 1975, Saturday 8:30-9:00pm

Episode#1: A Friend in Need - January 18, 1975 - Director: Jack Shea - Teleplay by: Don Nicholl, Michael Ross & Bernie West, Barry Harman & Harve Brosten - Story by: Barry Harman & Harve Brosten. Guest/s: Pauline Myers

The Jeffersons' success has gone to George's head. He is insisting that Louise hire a maid.

Episode#2: George's Family Tree - January 25, 1975 - Director: Jack Shea - Writer/s: Perry Grant & Dick Bensfield - Guest/s: No guests

George is very unimpressed about people's ancestors, until he finds out he is descended from a tribe of royalty.

Episode#3: Louise Feels Useless - February 1, 1975 - Director: Jack Shea - Writer/s: Lloyd Turner & Gordon Mitchell - Guest/s: Milton Selzer

Louise has nothing to do and decides to get a job without telling George.

Episode#4: Lionel the Playboy - February 8, 1975 - Director: Jack Shea - Writer/s: Roger Shulman & John Baskin - Guest/s: Ronnell Bright

Lionel is impressed with the family's new position in life and talks about quitting college.

Episode#5: Mr. Piano Man - February 15, 1975 - Director: Jack Shea - Writer/s: Don Nicholl and Lloyd Turner & Gordon Mitchell - Guest/s: Ivor Francis, Rozelle Gayle

George agrees to hold a tenant protest meeting in his apartment when he learns that the banker he's been trying to impress will be at the meeting.

Episode#6: George's Skeleton - February 22, 1975 - Director: Jack Shea - Writer/s: Lloyd Turner & Gordon Mitchell and Eric Tarloff - Guest/s: Moses Gunn

George's childhood pal shows up threatening to reveal George's past to his family unless George pays him off.

Episode#7: Lionel Cries Uncle - March 1, 1975 - Director: Jack Shea - Teleplay by: Lloyd Turner & Gordon Mitchell - Story by: Jim Carlson - Guest/s: Albert Reed and Ned Wertimer (Wertimer introduced as the doorman)

Louise is excited about her Uncle Ward coming to visit. George and Lionel are putting him down because they think he's an Uncle Tom.

Episode#8: Mother Jefferson's Boyfriend - March 8, 1975 - Director: Jack Shea - Writer/s: Gordon Farr & Arnold Kane - Guest/s: Alvin Childress, Ned Wertimer

Louise is excited when she learns Mother Jefferson has a boyfriend and may move to Florida, but George feels differently.

Episode#9: Meet the Press-March 15, 1975 - Director: Jack Shea - Writer/s: Dixie Brown Grossman - Guest/s: Carole Androsky, Bo Kaprall

George is convinced publicity will mean a boost to the cleaning business and therefore invites a member of the press to his home for an interview on his background.

Episode#10: Rich Man's Disease - March 22, 1975 - Director: Jack Shea - Writer/s: Bruce Howard - Guest/s: No guests

George has an ulcer and Louise is shielding him from anything that will upset him including her relationship with the Willises.

Episode#11: Former Neighbors - March 29, 1975 - Director: Jack Shea - Writer/s: Ben Joelson & Art Baer - Guest/s: Ernie Lee Banks, Maye Henderson, Santiago Gonzalez, Ned Wertimer

George is happy Louise has invited his old Harlem friends in for dinner until he learns she has invited them the same night he's having an influential businessman over.

Episode#12: Like Father, Like Son - April 5, 1975 - Director: Jack Shea - Writer/s: Frank Tarloff - Guest/s: No guests

Tom and George find themselves to be unexpected allies in a political campaign much to Helen Willis' disgust.

Episode#13: Jenny's Low - April 12, 1975 - Director: Jack Shea - Writer/s: John Ashby - Guest/s: Andrew Rubin (Rubin originated the role of Allan Willis, the eldest child of Tom and Helen Willis, but left the show during the first season) and Danny Wells (this episode introduced Wells as "Charlie" the bartender. He would go on to appear in 23 episodes ending with the June 4, 1985, episode.)

Jenny's brother returns suddenly after a two-year absence and is given an icy reception by his sister, who is angry because he has been passing for White. **(Interview with Berlinda Tolbert (Jenny) – Chapter Eighteen)**

At the end of Season One, in mutual agreement with Lear, Mike Evans left *The Jeffersons* to pursue other interests.

END OF SEASON ONE EPISODES
(At the end of each season's episode, Isabel Sanford is heard saying: *The Jeffersons* was recorded on tape in front of a live studio audience.)

From the first episode on January 18, 1975, until the last episode of the season, April 12, 1975, the program was in the top ten each week. To some, the show's popularity was surprising. Eight million Americans were unemployed, yet 35 million people watched *The Jeffersons* during this first season. It begins with the Jeffersons in a taxi on their way to their new apartment. Louise is crying and looking out the taxi window. This is where we get our first look at George's characteristic walk as they get out of the taxi and go into the building. George is forty-six and he and Louise have been married for twenty-five years. Morality lessons, realism, interracial marriage, stereotyping, racial equality, and the "shocking" use of Black slang was instrumental in *The Jeffersons* popularity.

Right off the bat, Marla Gibbs, as Florence, became a hit with her deliverance of a line that got a huge laugh from everyone in the studio, "How come we overcame, and nobody told me?" This line got the biggest laugh of the first episode. Kudos go to the writers. Marla Gibbs put just the right touch on that line. The right tone of voice. The right facial expression. A writer from *AP Television* agreed: "the only real laugh came at the end."

However, not all the critics who reviewed the show and reported their views were impressed with the characters or the scripts. Frank S. Swertlow of *Leader-Times*, Kittanning, Pennsylvania wrote: "And the acting by Hemsley and Sanford is too stiff. Unbelievable characters and poor dialogue." I must note here that the acting direction Sherman Hemsley received for the part of George Jefferson was that he be pompous and feisty. Pompous being synonymous with self-important, stiff, pontifical, haughty, arrogant, or grandiose. Hemsley played this part to the hilt.

This reporter, Jackie Gould of *Channel Chatter*, North Adams, Massachusetts, had issue with the family arguments: "It seems as if the Jeffersons are the argueingest (sic) family on TV." Yes, Norman Lear's sitcoms were known for being loud, with family disagreements being common with a bigot head of household in one (*All in the Family*) and lack of money the reason in the other (*Good Times*). According to Hemsley, the yelling and fighting was to attract viewer attention. The arguments were usually about how to use their money to enjoy their good fortune, like hiring a maid so Louise could go shopping. Louise's thoughts on the matter never seemed to quite gel with George's. Also, George was quite good at imparting his shortcomings to others, even Louise. Sanford's character had to be a strong, in-your-face character to be able to manage life with George. In fact, Sanford was quoted in the *Corsicana Daily Sun* saying: "Louise is the character who runs the show. In the end, I always get my way. He may think he gets his way, but he's in a dream world."

Some critics thought the writing on *The Jeffersons* was "loose and pedestrian." I say, "Au contraire." The writers used true to the character one-liners for George: for instance, when he is telling Weezy why she ought to have a maid to do her bidding he said, "Some people got to be the ma'ams and the rest are the mamees." This line fit the George Jefferson personality perfectly.

Lear knew his audience. In the first episode it is decided to have Tom and Helen kiss. In 1975 this was downright daring seeing that Tom was White, and Helen was Black. But they were married, and married people do kiss. Lear decided to take a chance and get it out of the way right at the beginning. The producers were ready for a barrage of complaints. According to Roker, CBS got four calls and two postcards, in total five were in favor of the kiss.

Interracial marriage had only been legal since about 1967 in the United States. But seeing it on television in 1975 was still groundbreaking. Today it is not even interesting. *The Jeffersons* at the time was shocking, incredulous, daring. Today some may see it as "quaint."

In the episode "Louise Feels Useless" Louise is unhappy living the life of the idle rich. She has a maid to do the housework and instead of being relieved and spending her days shopping, she wants to be productive. Seems that money has not solved all her problems. Also, George forbids her working. The word "forbids" does not sit well with Louise.

In creating this show, Lear was trying to portray an upwardly mobile Black family in a positive way that included humor. Sanford questioned how a prosperous Black family would be accepted by the general audience: "It will be interesting to see if the television viewers will accept a Black family that is upwardly mobile. I hope they do." It is unfortunate then that *The Afro-American Journal* had this to say in 1975: "The disheartening aspect of *The Jeffersons* is that the film confirms the stereotype of the black as greedy, stupid, egotistical, frivolous, irresponsible, incompetent, and wants to be like the white man in every respect. This series is very bad."

Because the idea for *The Jeffersons* stemmed directly from a visit from the Black Panther's Organization, this series is just what the doctor ordered. The newspaper article seems to imply truth in the stereotype that all Blacks want to be "like the White man." If we fast-forward to 1979, Gibbs had this to say in a *TV Guide* interview: "I feel we break out of stereotypes. I'm bucking the Establishment; they can't rule me. I don't take any guff."

The Jeffersons featured Black characters who had a thriving business, through responsible actions. Had George Jefferson been frivolous he would not have moved-on-up and stupidity had nothing to do with his success as a Black man. Rather than wanting to be like the White man, George wanted a better life for himself and his family. George Jefferson was proud of being a Black man who had worked hard and raised himself up from poverty to owning a successful business.

The theme song "Movin' On Up" spells it out perfectly with these words: "Took a <u>whole</u> lotta tryin' just to get up that hill. Now we're up in the big leagues, gettin' our turn at bat. As long as we live, it's you and me baby, there ain't <u>nothin'</u> wrong with that." They finally got a piece of the pie, which, in my humble opinion, is what most of us want.

The first season brought in award winning guests. In "George's Skeleton" the guest was Moses Gunn, whose extensive career included at that time, off-Broadway and Broadway productions. He performed Shakespearean roles, winning two Obie awards for his portrayal as Aaron, in *Titus Andronicus* and for his role in *First Breeze of Summer* which would go on to Broadway. He had also performed as Othello at the Stratford, Connecticut Shakespeare Festival. Gunn's background included film and television work. He appeared in the films *Nothing but a Man*, *The Great White Hope*, and *Shaft*, to name a few, and in the TV series *Kung Fu* and *Hawaii Five-O*.

Actors who had been in the entertainment business since the early 1930s, like Alvin Childress, were brought in which helped keep their talents before the public. In the episode titled "Mother Jefferson's Boyfriend," the boyfriend in question was played by Childress, an actor with many years of experience. Childress was probably best known as Amos Jones, the cabdriver in the 1951 television sitcom *Amos 'n Andy*. Childress had performed with Harlem's Lafayette Players, the Federal Theater Project, and the American Negro Project. He appeared in a number of 1930 and 1940 stage productions, including *Savage Rhythm*, *Brown Sugar*, *The Case of Phillip Lawrence*, *Anna Lucasta*, and *The Amen Corner*. His film credits include *Hell's Alley*, *Harlem is Heaven*, *Dixie Love*, *Anna Lucasta* and *Thunderbolt and Lightfoot*, to name just a few. He was also in a 1972 episode of *Sanford and Son*.

One of my favorite episodes during this season was "Mr. Piano Man." George graciously consents to having a tenant meeting in his apartment, but, of course, he had intentions of impressing the owner of the building, so he ordered a piano for his apartment. Unfortunately, the piano was too large for the living room and left little space for the guests. When George saw the piano, he lost his cool. He wants it out of there! The piano delivery man, played by Rozelle Gayle, returns with the piano seat not knowing there is a problem. Gayle was a big, tall, gruff-looking man and in character he looked unkempt, clashing with George's meeting attendees who had dressed for the occasion, which of course meant the two men clashed. The doorbell rings and George, thinking it is Whittendale, tries to rush to the door, through the crowd in his apartment, past the piano while Florence is trying to do the same. This episode was super funny and included a fantastic slapstick spot with George getting so aggravated with Florence he puts his hands around her neck as if to choke her. The new visitor was Whittendale's representative, and it is discovered he is familiar with the piano man who plays jazz at the local club, which leads to a somewhat chastened George Jefferson who had been condescending while dealing with the piano man.

I decided to do some research on Gayle for this book and learned that he was not only a comedian who had recorded at least two comic albums, but that he was also an accomplished pianist who played everything from boogie to Bach. Before appearing on *The Jeffersons*, Gayle had appeared on film in *The Joint is Jumpin'* (1948) and *The Devil's Daughter* (1978), a made for TV movie, and would go on to other TV and movie roles.

During this season one of the biggest issues was how African Americans allowed themselves to be portrayed. The episode "Lionel Cries Uncle" displayed positivity regarding racial equality and affection among family members. Louise's Uncle Ward, played by Albert Reed, comes to visit. Uncle Ward is employed as a servant to a wealthy White man, so George and Lionel make fun of him by calling him Uncle Tom. Uncle Ward straightens the two out, pointing out how even someone who does a menial job deserves others' respect if he is competent in his job. "The network, production company and I got more response from that show than any others. It was so educational," said Reed.

The writers in this show must have had good rapport with the cast, because some of these lines are almost insulting, but so true. George is reading a newspaper about a man who saves a wino from being mugged. George guesses that the wino was White because the paper called the wino indigent. He said: "White winos go to the Salvation Army and are indigent and Black winos get busted and are inmates." In the real world this is a truth. The sitcom presents it in a way that people can laugh at the ridiculousness.

In "Meet the Press," George is about to be interviewed about his rise to success. When taking a call from a press office he pretends to be the butler answering the phone. He uses a different voice. A sort of watered-down Stepin Fetchit voice. Watching this today, I clearly saw this being a way to suggest that the butler was "colored." I was a bit surprised, no, I was shocked that Hemsley chose to go along with that impression as it was clearly racist. However, I laughed out loud. If I had been with someone while I was watching this, I would have used a current term: "No he didn't!"

If I had been watching this in 1975, I may not have caught the mimic, especially as the show came on at 8:30 p.m. I was a single, working mom and would have seriously been considering settling in for the night. At that time, I watched the show because it had a mostly Black cast, and it was silly, funny, and sometimes outrageous. But today in 2021 when I have taken a good look at our Black History I can see more clearly. *The Jeffersons* was a truly risk taking or should I say daring, television show.

During 1975, an article appeared in *The News*, of Port Arthur, Texas, that stated there was "no story to *The Jeffersons* - no point, no moral." Having recently looked at the early Season One episodes I can say that there were, in fact, points made, and morality lessons learned, as in "Like Father, Like Son." Lionel resorts to acting like his father to get his way, using lies, rudeness, and shouting. When George finds out, he is fine with Lionel's actions. Louise thinks Lionel is ok without resorting to his father's ways. George's retort shows his thinking regarding Blacks and Whites in their current world; he says that "OK" is not good enough for a Jefferson and that "Ok is only good for tall, blond kids with blue eyes."

The Jeffersons was true to the times. The cast members were free to ad-lib phrases to add a sense of realism. Phrases that today cannot be uttered on television but were used widely by society at the time and are still being used. For instance, one episode has George spending $350 on a watch for Lionel. Louise could not believe it! And to make a point, she says "Three hundred and fifty dollars for a watch! Nigga, please!" I laughed out loud in total agreement. My mother would probably have said "Are you for real?" or today someone might say "Shut the front door!" I would have said "OKAY?!" In other words, Louise was expressing her displeasure at the large amount of money George chose to spend on a watch. The term itself was familiar to the viewing audience in 1975. In the context of the show, it was understood that there was no animosity involved, just incredulity at George's action. It is banned from use on television today. The scene got a loud laugh from the studio audience.

The Jeffersons TV sitcom was much more than a TV show with a loud decibel level and people bickering with no point to the episodes. The Jeffersons were loud, no doubt about that. Lear knew his audience, and he knew what worked. The sitcom was relatable, groundbreaking, and funny. Possibly, the critics who could not see this in the episodes were watching through angry eyes or, perhaps, in those early days, critics were looking for this show to fail.

Of course, during this first season, there were some folks who believed Norman Lear had another hit on his hands. Arthur Unger of *The Christian Science Monitor*, San Rafael, California, wrote, "In typical Lear fashion, the show has strong concepts, skillful writing, hard-edged humor, and fine ensemble acting." The phrase "skillful writing" is key. In watching these TV sitcoms, it is easy to forget that these actors are performing from written scripts.

I sent out queries online asking people what they thought about the character in another book I am writing. One lady said she loved the character's outspokenness and how she interacted with her family. Another responder replied to her comment saying the actor was simply saying the writer's words and that no one ever gave the writers credit. I replied that the actor's ability to bring the writing to life is what enabled the show to be successful. The writers and the actors were members of a family.

Zara Cully was a good example of this as Mother Jefferson. She was an audience favorite from the first episode. One reviewer described her character as "refreshingly non-understanding, non-sympathetic and definitely not nice to her daughter-in-law." She was a true acting professional. *The Jeffersons* used good actors and relevant issues, with positivity and humor, to entertain their viewing audience.

In early February, Sanford was interviewed in Corsicana, Texas about being a Black female on television in a major role: "This is something I never expected to see in my lifetime. Why, we were beneath the totem pole when I started in the American Negro Theater."

Actors are happy to have work like anyone else. In the 1970s Black actors were few and far between on television. It was difficult to realize their dream. Once that dream begins it is easy to get carried away on that cloud of fame. Sanford kept her humility as you can see in her remarks to *The Daily Independent* of Kannapolis, North Carolina, "I have to laugh when people refer to me as a star. The word star is not important to me. If there is a star, it is *The Jeffersons*."

The actors also brought positive attitudes when they showed up for work. When they did the show about Jenny's White-looking brother returning, the producers wanted Roker's character to show favoritism to Jenny since both had the same skin color. According to the *Mansfield, Ohio News Journal*, Roker said she handed the script right back to the producers, telling them she "couldn't play that" since she was a mother and would not treat any of her children that way.

The life of an actor can be busy on and off the set. People want to see them in person to get an autograph or have their picture taken with a "star." During the 1975 summer hiatus *The Jeffersons* TV family appeared at The Ebony Masters Fashion Show and Celebrity Auction held at Martin Luther King, Jr. Community Center, in Los Angeles; Hemsley appeared on *Joey and Dad*; Tolbert was honored at the Festival of Arts given by Berkley Alumnae Chapter of Delta Sigma Theta at the Oakland Auditorium Theater and Sanford appeared on the *Tony Orlando and Dawn* TV show.

Of course, *The Jeffersons* popularity that year would not have been complete without seeing George and Louise celebrating Thanksgiving. On November 27, 1975, CBS televised the All-American Thanksgiving Day Parade featuring highlights from five parades. Hemsley and Sanford were chosen to be commentators from Macy's in Philadelphia for their 56th annual Gimbel's Thanksgiving Parade.

Fast forwarding to 2007, Lester D. Friedman is looking back at "American Cinema of the 1970s: Themes and Variations" and he references *The Jeffersons*. "Although critics complained that the show simply recycled racial stereotypes, the fact that its cast was predominantly African American, that it showcased an upwardly mobile African American family living in a predominantly White neighborhood, and that it featured an interracial couple all combined to demonstrate a new attitude in the country, though perhaps its limits as well. The show represented both how far Americans had traveled along the road to racial equality and, to some extent, also confirmed the seemingly insurmountable obstacles that lay before them." *Rutgers University Press*, New Brunswick, NJ, 2007.

In a 2016 interview with CBS news, Lear said: "I didn't think we were pushing an envelope, I thought we were dealing with the problems American families were facing." Lear did just that. I found this 2020 article in *The Atlantic* magazine written by an immigrant to the United States. The title of the article was "What *The Jeffersons* Taught Me About Being an American." The writer of the article said that George and Louise reminded him of his parents, George, the hardworking head of household and Louise as the moral anchor. He said George's actions taught him about survival. He even liked George's trash-talking because it reminded him of the home he left behind.

Chapter Six:
Season Two

Episode#14: A Dinner for Harry - September 13, 1975 - Director: Jack Shea - Writer/s: Don Nicholl, Michael Ross, & Bernie West - Guest/s: Marla Gibbs, Ned Wertimer, Ben Rizzi, Richard Libertini, Zackie Cooper

Louise's birthday party for Bentley hits a snag when Tom Willis decides to move his family from New York, after learning that his wife Helen was mugged.

Episode#15: George's First Vacation - September 20, 1975 - Jack Shea - Writer/s: Frank Tarloff - Guest/s: No guests

George, convinced by Louise and the Willises that he's a workaholic and needs a vacation, decides to take Louise on a cruise.

Episode#16: Louise's Daughter - September 27, 1975 - Director: Jack Shea, Writer/s: Jay Moriarty & Mike Milligan (Moriarty and Milligan met in a comedy writing workshop. According to Jay Moriarty in his book "Honkey in the House," the two became official writing partners on St. Patrick's Day, March 17, 1973. Their first paid assignment in 1974 was a script for *Good Times*. By 1975 Moriarty and Milligan were staff writers for *The Jeffersons*. Moriarty also discusses the question of how White writers can write for Black shows, "I write comedy.") - Guest/s: Diane Sommerfield and Danny Wells

Louise and George are shocked when a strange girl shows up at their door saying she has documents proving that she is Louise's daughter.

Time Slot Change: September 1975-October 1976, from Saturday 8:30-9:00pm to Saturday 8:00-8:30pm

Episode#17: Harry & Daphne - October 4, 1975 - Director: Jack Shea - Writer/s: Lloyd Turner & Gordon Mitchell - Guest/s: Rene Auberjonois, Melinda Dillon

Bentley involves the Jeffersons when he tries to avoid what he thinks is a marriage proposal from his girlfriend.

Episode#18: Mother Jefferson's Fall - October 11, 1975 - Director: Jack Shea - Writer/s: Erik Tarloff - Guest/s: Dorothy Butts, Estelle Evans, Maidie Norman, Ruth Lee, Hilda Haynes, Ned Wertimer

Mother Jefferson feels neglected and fakes a back injury to get attention from everyone.

Episode#1 9: Jefferson vs. Jefferson - October 18, 1975 - Director: Jack Shea - Writer/s: Robert Fisher & Arthur Marx - Guest/s: Ned Wertimer

Louise puts her foot down when George expects her to lie for him after he is involved in a bicycle accident in the park.

Episode#20: Uncle Bertram - October 25, 1975 - Director: Jack Shea - Writer/s: Don Nicholl, Michael Ross & Bernie West, and Lloyd Turner & Gordon Mitchell – Guest/s: Ned Wertimer, Victor Kilian

George objects to the friendship between Mother Jefferson and Tom Willis' uncle.

Episode#21: Movin' On Down - November 1, 1975 - Director: Jack Shea - Writer/s: Ken Levine & David Isaacs - Guest/s: No guests

George is depressed because he feels his business setbacks will change his way of living.

Episode#22: George Won't Talk - November 8, 1975 - Director: Jack Shea - Writer/s: John Ashby - Guests/s: Robert Guillaume and Ernest L. Thomas **(See Interview with Ernest L. Thomas - Chapter Eighteen)**

George is excited when he is invited to speak at a college but tries to get out of it when he learns the college is in the ghetto.

Episode#23: Jenny's Grandparents - November 15, 1975 - Director: Jack Shea - Writer/s: James Ritz - Guest/s: Leon Ames, Fred Pinkard, Victor Killian

Mother Jefferson and Uncle Bertram join forces to bring together the feuding fathers of Tom and Helen Willis.

Episode#24: George's Best Friend - November 22, 1975 - Director: Jack Shea – Teleplay by: Calvin Kelly and Lloyd Turner & Gordon Mitchell - Story by: Calvin Kelly - Guest/s: Louis Gossett, Jr.

George's old buddy from his Navy days shows up at the house. George is delighted to see him, but Louise has a different reaction when he makes a pass at her when George isn't around.

Episode#25: George and the Manager - November 29, 1975 - Director: Jack Shea - Teleplay by Don Boyle and Jay Moriarty & Mike Milligan - Story by: Don Boyle - Guest/s: Norma Donaldson, Rhoda Gemignani

George needs a manager for one of his cleaning stores, but is reluctant to promote a qualified employee because she is a woman.

Episode#26: George's Alibi - December 6, 1975 - Director: Jack Shea - Writer/s: Sandy Krinski - Guest/s: Ned Wertimer, Tom Brown (voice only)

George, not knowing that Lionel bashed in the fender of the new delivery van, thinks he hit someone while driving home from work at night.

Episode#27: Lunch with Mama - December 13, 1975 - Director: Jack Shea - Writer/s: Don Nichol, Michael Ross & Bernie West, and Lloyd Turner & Gordon Mitchell - Guest/s: J. A. Preston

There is turmoil in the Jefferson house when Louise asks George to attend a funeral with her on the same day Mother Jefferson is expecting him to take her to lunch.

Episode#28: George vs. Wall Street - December 20, 1975 - Director: Jack Shea - Writer/s: George Burditt - Guest/s: Ned Wertimer

George's success in the futures market is marred when he learns Lionel has turned down a $20,000 a year job.

Episode#29: The Break-Up, Pt. 1 - January 3, 1976 - Director: Jack Shea - Writer/s: Dixie Brown Grossman - Guest/s: No guests

War breaks out between the Jeffersons and the Willises when George buys Lionel a term paper. When Lionel decides to use it, Jenny breaks off their engagement.

Episode#30: The Break-Up, Pt. 2 - January 10, 1976 - Director: Jack Shea - Writer/s: Lloyd Turner & Gordon Mitchell - Guest/s: Marion Ramsey, Ned Wertimer

With Lionel and Jenny broken up, George introduces his son to a beautiful Black girl, not knowing that her profession is the world's oldest!

Episode#31: Florence's Problem - January 24, 1976 - Director: Jack Shea - Writer/s: Jay Moriarty & Mike Milligan - No Guest/s

The Jeffersons are shocked when they learn their maid, Florence, is planning suicide.

Episode#32: Mother Jefferson's Birthday - January 31, 1976 - Director: Jack Shea - Writer/s: Fred S. Fox & Seaman Jacobs - Guest/s: Lillian Randolph

George and Louise surprise Mother Jefferson by inviting her sister Emma, whom she has not talked to in twenty-five years, to celebrate her "special" birthday.

Episode#33: Louise's Cookbook - February 7, 1976 - Director: Jack Shea - Teleplay by Jay Moriarty & Mike Milligan and Gordon Mitchell & Lloyd Turner - Story by Ann Gibbs & Joel Kimmel - Guest/s: Robert Lussier

Louise is thrilled when a publisher asks her to write a cookbook of her grandmother's old recipes. George, however, is not crazy about the idea.

Episode#34: George Meets Whittendale - February 14, 1976 - Director: Jack Shea - Writer/s: Lloyd Turner & Gordon Mitchell - Guest/s: Ned Wertimer

George's big chance to meet Whittendale, the banker, is foiled when he is accidently locked in his guest bathroom with the Willises and can't get out.

Episode#35: Lionel's Problem - February 21, 1976 - Director: Jack Shea - Teleplay by: James Ritz - Story by: Mea Abbott - Guest/s: No guest/s

Louise finds out that Lionel, afraid he won't live up to his father's expectations, gets drunk on his graduation day. She, Mother Jefferson, and Jenny keep Lionel away from George until he sobers up.

Episode#36: Tennis, Anyone? - February 28, 1976 - Director: Jack Shea - Writer/s: Sandy Veith - Guest/s: Keene Curtis, Davis Roberts, Ray Sharkey

George is all set to join an exclusive tennis club until he learns he has been invited to join only to be the "token Black."

Episode#37: The Wedding - March 6, 1976 - Director: Jack Shea - Writer/s: John Donley, Lloyd Turner & Gordon Mitchell - Guest/s: Bobby Johnson, Nick La Tour, Ned Wertimer

George and Louise plan to renew their marriage vows and all goes well until the wedding day when they have a difference of opinions over George's prices in his Harlem store.

END OF SEASON TWO EPISODES

Season Two began on September 13, 1975. *The Jeffersons* had a strong start as a spin-off of *AITF*, but by the start of this season, the show had lost its lead as the No. 4 spot and plummeted to No. 13.

The part of Lionel is now played by Damon Evans (no relation to Mike), as Mike Evans had left the show to pursue other interests. In a December 1975 interview, Damon Evans is quoted as saying, "I always wanted to work with Norman Lear. He educates his audiences. It's still a situation comedy, but the situations are real." Evans fit in well, even though he had never seen an episode of *The Jeffersons*.

How the show toppled from a top spot in one season is a mystery to me. The writing was funny, and the actors were professional and intent on providing the television viewers with a reason to keep tuning in. Season Two tackled a few tough family issues, though laughter was still in the mix, with an emphasis on community involvement. I must give kudos to the writers and to the producers, and to the casting people for their choice of actors.

The "Mother Jefferson's Fall" episode was hilarious. Mother Jefferson has a bright idea after an uncomfortable exchange with George, who seems to be ignoring her presence. Before huffing off into the kitchen she tells him: "Well, excuse me for living." Her bright idea was to pretend to have a fall in the kitchen which brings George and Louise running. She is found out in the end when she invites her girlfriends over for tea and George finds her walking around the room modeling her new dressing gown.

I laughed out loud through this whole episode. The cast in this episode included Dorothy Butts, who had appeared in *The Doctors* (1967-1976), Estelle Evans, who appeared in a 1948 documentary *The Quiet One* and in *To Kill A Mockingbird* (1967); Ruth Lee who had been in acting since 1967, and Hilda Haynes. One other guest, Maidie Norman, was, and probably still is, a familiar face. Norman began acting in 1947 in *The Peanut Man*, and her TV show appearances included *The Jack Benny Show*, *Dragnet*, *Alfred Hitchcock Presents*, *Ben Casey*, *The Twilight Zone*, *Hazel*, *The Man from U.N.C.L.E.* and many others. She also appeared in the 1962 movie *What Ever Happened to Baby Jane*. The casting of the guests in this episode added greatly to my enjoyment because between them they had years of experience in their craft.

Casting is a major part of producing a successful program. As an example, casting Marla Gibbs as Florence Johnston was brilliant. The fact that the Jeffersons had a maid who had no trouble challenging her employer kept the audience tuning in every week. Throughout the series her sassiness and back-talking was a crowd-pleasing attraction.

George: You makin' poached salmon?

Florence: Yea, any objections?!

Another example of great casting was using legendary actors as guests. In "Mother Jefferson's Birthday" this is done with a visit from her sister Emma, played by Lillian Randolph. Emma shows up as a surprise, after a call from George, because the two women had been estranged for twenty-five years. When the sisters see each other, they are both overcome with joy. Unfortunately, Emma mentions that she couldn't stay away from her sister's 75th birthday. Mother Jefferson's reaction is priceless. Mother Jefferson had told everyone she was 70 years old which means the two sisters began to bicker. However, she finally proudly admits to being three-quarters of a century.

As I look back at this episode, I am a bit disappointed. I noticed that Lillian Randolph did not get a welcoming applause from the studio audience the way Sammy Davis, Jr. did in Season Ten. When

Randolph began acting, Davis was only five years old. Her resume was extensive, but it seems like she did not get special notice from *The Jeffersons* audience.

I came across Lillian Randolph's biography while researching a biography on my father, Eddie Green in 2015, because her sister Amanda Randolph had appeared in one of my father's movies, *Comes Midnight* (1939). Lillian Randolph, born in 1914, had enjoyed an extensive career in the entertainment business though she was not often spoken about. She was an actor and singer, a veteran of radio, film, and television, appearing in hundreds of shows. She is best remembered today for her role in the movie *It's a Wonderful Life* (1947) (she contributed the money she was saving for a "deevorce" to a fund for George Bailey). In March 1980, she was inducted into the Black Filmmakers Hall of Fame. She died on September 12, 1980.

Speaking of well-known actors, in "George Won't Talk" Robert Guillaume made a guest appearance as Mr. Johnson, a man who wanted George to give an inspirational talk to a group of Harlem youngsters who needed guidance. Ernest L. Thomas portrayed "Train" a gang leader who had ripped off one of the trucks from George's cleaning business.

Guillaume was an already well-known Broadway performer who had toured the world as a cast member in the Broadway musical *Free and Easy*, and had appeared on stage with Sammy Davis, Jr. in *Golden Boy*. In 1964 he played "Sportin' Life" in a revival of *Porgy and Bess*, and he played the Phantom in the 1990 Los Angeles production of *The Phantom of the Opera*.

Thomas went from appearing on this episode to winning the role of Roger "Raj" Thomas on the TV sitcom *What's Happening*. **(See Interview with Ernest Thomas - Chapter Eighteen)**

"George's Old Friend" Wendell Brown, played by Louis Gossett, Jr., provided a reason for the producers to take a chance in this one. I was told that the cast members had the choice to ad lib when they felt it was appropriate. George's old friend turns up to visit and is invited to stay a while. When George's old navy buddy finds Louise at home alone, he gets a bit too "touchy feely." After telling Louise he knows a "no" means yes, he grabs her. Mother Jeffersons comes in from the bedroom, picks up an umbrella and begins to hit him with it. George walks in and when he finds out that Wendell was making passes at Louise, he is incredulous. He blurts out "Nigger, you got to be crazy! Now I know you done backdoored lots of people, but I didn't think you'd be stupid enough to try to backdoor me. Sucker, you'd better get out of my house before I erase your future."

This situation called for a drastic reaction. It called for anger. George's "old buddy" was way out of place, and Hemsley's character, George, as a Black man in the 1970s, reacted as expected by letting Wendell Brown know, in no uncertain terms, that he had just crossed the line. What I have been told from those present at the time is that the audience responded with clapping and verbal agreement. This was the truth of the real world at the time. This was an ad-lib by Hemsley, not read from a script, but it put some realism into the scene. The word is not always used in anger. Sometimes it is meant as a greeting, or as a way of addressing a longtime friend, or as they might say today, a "homeboy." Today, in 2021 the word is still very much in use, no matter how much insistence there is to not use "the n-word." Take a walk around your city. Visit a High School. Ride public transportation. Listen to certain music. Though we bleep it now on television and radio, there is no way to muzzle a human being's speech or to restrain a person from writing what they mean to say.

If we are going to be upset by something, how about tackling the problem of suicide. A deep issue that is not funny, but that *The Jeffersons* figured out how to approach with tact and humor. "Florence's Problem" has her feeling alone and non-productive and she decides she is "Going to be with the Lord. Oh Hallelujah!" The episode starts off with an exchange between George and Florence. Louise is reading a question from a magazine to George: "If a man wears a size 34 belt what size suspenders does he wear?" Florence answers the question: "Any fool could answer that." George retorts: "I know, but I ain't asking you."

Through a misunderstanding, the whole family comes to believes that Florence is going to jump off the Empire State Building. But before they can locate her to stop her, she comes home. She tells them why her predicament is leading her to want to leave this world, that she is alone and has no friends. Lionel tells her: "We are your friends. Don't you see you're more to us than just a maid?" Given that Florence always has something smart to say, she replies: "Lord, I thought Black folks only heard that from White folks." Hugs and tears ensue.

As the season closed, the cast members were kept busy appearing as guests on shows like *The Rich Little Show* where Hemsley shared the stage with Tom Bosley and Lawrence Hilton Jacobs. He also went on tour starring with Andre Pavon in an interracial version of *The Odd Couple*. On the *Donny & Marie Show*, Hemsley performed in a western sketch with Donny, Jim Connell, and Ruth Buzzi. Playing the part of George Jefferson had made Hemsley quite popular. TV watchers could also catch him on *The Sonny & Cher Show* where he did a comedy sketch as Mervin the Magician.

At an event sponsored by the Metropolitan Church of Altadena, cast member Berlinda Tolbert was among the celebrities to entertain after an outreach banquet at Pasadena Conference Center; and as a top off for this summer hiatus, Roxie Roker was honored by the Howard University with the 1976 Alumni Award for "distinguished postgraduate achievement in the field of the Performing Arts."

Due to the popularity of *The Jeffersons*, the program was even being mentioned in local housing ads. On August 22, 1976, an article appeared in a real estate ad by *Town & Country* in three different newspapers. To quote part of the ad… "*The Jeffersons* would love the spaciousness of this 2-story, 3 bedrooms, finished basement." Obviously, it was assumed that everybody knew about *The Jeffersons*.

Chapter Seven:
Season Three

Episode#38: George and the President - September 25, 1976 - Director: Jack Shea - Writer/s: Howard Albrecht & Sol Weinstein - Guest/s: David Dukes, Nick LaTour

George hires an advertising man to do a campaign that will bring him more business in his cleaning stores. The ad man's idea is to pass George off as Thomas Jefferson's Great-great-great-grandson.

Episode#39: Louise Gets Her Way - October 2, 1976 - Director: Jack Shea - Writer/s: Lloyd Turner & Gordon Mitchell - Guest/s: Richard Mckenzie, Ned Wertimer

Florence is without a place to live, and Louise decides to hire her as a live-in maid. George is against the idea.

Episode#40: Louise Suspects - October 9, 1976 - Director: Jack Shea - Writer/s: Lloyd Turner & Gordon Mitchell - No guests

George is opening another cleaning store and does not want Louise to know. He is acting so suspicious and secretive; Louise thinks he is having an affair with another woman.

Episode#41: The Lie Detector - October 16, 1976 - Director: Jack Shea - Writer/s: Tedd Anasti & David Talisman - Guest/s: Arny Freeman, Tom Lacy, Mason McCalman

Lionel turns down a job as an engineer because the company requires all employees take a lie detector test.

Episode#42: George's Diploma - October 23, 1976 - Director: Jack Shea - Writer/s: Lloyd Turner & Gordon Mitchell - No guests

George, thinking that Lionel is ashamed of him because he never graduated from high school, decides to get his diploma by taking an Equivalency Test for adults.

Episode#43: Retirement Party - October 30, 1976 - Director: Jack Shea - Writer/s: Dixie Brown Grossman - Guest/s: Richard Ward

George is all set to sell his cleaning stores to a conglomerate, but there is one problem. The company's rule that all employees must retire at the age of 60 means that Ben, George's longtime friend and manager of his main store, must retire because he is 63.

Time Slot Change: November 1976 - January 1977, from Saturday 8:00-8:30pm to Wednesday 8:00-8:30pm

Episode#44: Lionel's Pad - November 10, 1976 - Director: Jack Shea - Writer/s: Booker Bradshaw & Kurt Taylor - No guests

Lionel has taken an apartment and Jenny is moving in with him. Both the Jeffersons and the Willises are against the idea.

Episode#45: Tom the Hero - November 17, 1976 - Director: Jack Shea - Writer/s: Jay Moriarty & Mike Milligan - Guest/s: Ed Cambridge, Mickey Deems, Ned Wertimer

Tom saves George's life, and no one is letting George forget it.

Episode#46: Jenny's Discovery - November 24, 1976 - Director: Jack Shea - Writer/s: Bob Baublitz - Guest/s: Bob Duggan, Ginny Tyler, Mickey Deems

Jenny has doubts about her feelings for Lionel until she thinks that he has been involved in a bus crash and may be dead.

Episode#47: The Agreement - December 8, 1976 - Director: Jack Shea - Writer/s: Lloyd Turner & Gordon Mitchell - Guest/s: Paul Barselou

Jenny and Lionel call off their wedding over a misunderstanding about a prenuptial agreement George thinks Jenny should sign.

Episode#48: Florence in Love - December 15, 1976 - Director: Jack Shea - Teleplay by: Richard Freiman & Stephen Young - Story by: Paul M. Belous & Robert Wolterstorff - Guest/s: Robert DoQui

Florence quits her job when George and Louise object to her boyfriend spending the night at their apartment.

Episode#49: The Christmas Wedding - December 22, 1976 - Director: Jack Shea - Writer/s: Jay Moriarty & Mike Milligan - Guest/s: Ned Wertimer, Robert Sampson

George and Tom Willis almost come to blows over the arrangements for the kids' wedding. Louise decides to solve everything by having the ceremony at the Jefferson apartment. It is performed under George and Tom's noses, and they are not aware what's happening!

Time Slot Change: January 1977 - August 1977, from Wednesday 8:00-8:30pm to Monday 8:00-8:30pm

Episode#50: Louise Forgets - January 5, 1977 - Director: Jack Shea - Writer/s: Bill Davenport - Guest/s: Ned Wertimer

Although Louise is studying a book on how to improve her memory, she still forgets to give George's stockbroker an order. George hits the ceiling when he finds out her "memory" cost him $20,000.

Episode#51: Bentley's Problem - January 12, 1977 - Director: Jack Shea - Writer/s: Lloyd Turner & Gordon Mitchell - Guest/s: Paul Larson, Alan Manson

George tries to help Bentley solve his problem with a nasty neighbor, but only makes matters worse and Bentley winds up in jail!

Episode#52: Jefferson Airplane - January 17, 1977 - Director: Jack Shea - Teleplay by: Dixie Brown Grossman - Story by: Brian Levant - Guest/s: Conrad Janis, Billy Sands

Louise suggests George take up a hobby. He decides on flying and is excited about it until he gets airsick his first time up.

Episode#53: George's Guilt - January 24, 1977 - Director: Jack Shea - Writer/s: Jay Moriarty & Mike Milligan - Guest/s: Henry Harris, Bill Henderson, Les Weaver

George tries to renew friendships with his childhood buddies by inviting them to his house for a reunion.

Episode#54: A Case of Black and White - January 31, 1977 - Director: Jack Shea - Writer/s: Fred S. Fox & Seaman Jacobs and Lloyd Turner & Gordon Mitchell - Guest/s: Ned Wertimer, Barbara Carson, J. Jay Saunders

In trying to win over a potential business associate, a Black man married to a White woman, George invites the Willises and the Howards to dinner and is on his best behavior.

Episode#55: Louise vs. Jenny - February 7, 1977 - Director: Jack Shea - Writer/s: John Ashby - Guest/s: Ned Wertimer

When Lionel falls sick at the Jefferson house, Louise and Jenny almost come to blows as to who should take care of him and where.

Episode#56: The Marriage Counselors - February 21, 1977 - Director: Jack Shea - Writer/s: John V. Hanrahan - No guests

The Willises, blissfully happy after taking a Marriage Improvement course, try to teach the willing Louise and reluctant George how to improve their marriage.

Episode#57: Louise's Friend - February 28, 1977 - Director: Jack Shea - Writer/s: Teleplay by: Richard Freiman & Stephen Young and Jay Moriarty & Mike Milligan - Story by Richard Freimand & Stephen Young - Guest/s: Hal Williams, and S. Pearl Sharpe

When Louise's friend comes to take her to their French class, George has a fit when the friend turns out to be an attractive man.

Episode#58: The Old Flame - March 7, 1977 - Director: Jack Shea - Writer/s: Jay Moriarty & Mike Milligan - Guest/s: Lillian Lehman

Mother Jefferson invites George's first girlfriend to dinner and the minute Louise's back is turned; the old flame makes a play for unsuspecting George.

Episode#59: Jenny's Opportunity - March 21, 1977 - Director: Jack Shea - Teleplay by: Lloyd Turner & Gordon Mitchell - Story by: Paul M. Belous & Robert Wolterstorff - No guests

Jenny's winning a summer scholarship to Oxford creates problems between her and Lionel and their respective families.

Episode#60: George the Philanthropist - March 28, 1977 - Director: Jack Shea - Writer: Dennis Koenig & Larry Balmagia - Guest/s: Ernest Harden, Jr., Henry G. Sanders, and Lester Phillips

I caught up with Ernest Harden, Jr. whose character began as Jason King in this his first appearance on *The Jeffersons*. He would later appear in a recurring role as Marcus Henderson. **(See Interview with Ernest Harden, Jr. - Chapter Eighteen)**

George's scheme to win the Black Businessman Association's award by donating $3000.00 to reopen a youth center in Harlem backfires.

Episode#61: Louise's Physical - April 11, 1977 - Director: Jack Shea - Writer/s: Lloyd Turner & Gordon Mitchell and Jay Moriarty

& Mike Milligan - Guest/s: Rhonda Cunningham, C. Lindsay Workman

George is trying to throw a surprise birthday party for Louise and Louise is depressed because she feels she is not doing anything worthwhile with her life.

END OF SEASON THREE EPISODES

Jealousy, marital disagreements, and bad advice is the order of this season, with the usual hilarity, love and some forgiveness thrown in. Clips of scenes from the last two seasons flash by before the show begins. Zara Cully, who plays the character of Mother Jefferson, missed the first 17 episodes of this season due to illness. Cully wanted to be back at work, and when she reported for it, she never missed a line during the taping of the episode.

During this season there were two time slot changes. In November, the show moved from Saturday 8:00-8:30 p.m. to Wednesday from 8:00-8:30 p.m. and in January of 1977 it moved to Monday from 8:00-8:30 p.m. Was this better or worse for ratings? An Ohio journalist wrote in January 1978, *The Jeffersons* was "one of the best comedies on television today." Looking back, it seems that *The Jeffersons* was on a roller-coaster ride of success. The show began by climbing to the top, then dropping quickly during the second season only to rise again in Season Three.

By September 1976, *The Jeffersons* had won the lead-off spot in Saturday comedy night on CBS. Perhaps it was the wonderful guests. Maybe it was because Florence had become a permanent cast member, or maybe it was because the writers had improved their already well-honed writing skills. In his book *Honkey in the House*, Jay Moriarty writes (in the third person) about what he thought of the matter: "In retrospect, as much as Murph liked to export relevance and destroy stereotypes, he was still, in his very DNA, about finding the funny."

In Season Three *The Jeffersons* was still funny, especially when Florence is around. Funny and surprising. In "Louise Gets Her Way" George does not like their maid, Florence. She talks back and comes to work late.

George: Do you know how late you are?

Florence: Why? Did I miss something?

She seems to have no respect for the fact that he is her boss. Due to Florence having to move out of her apartment with nowhere to go, Louise hires her as a live-in maid. But George puts his foot down and fires Florence. Later that afternoon Florence saves George from being a "pigeon" in a risky business deal and George is so happy he re-hires her. He also grabs her and lands two or three kisses on her cheeks! What a great ending!

The idea of anyone being able to intrude on a person's private thoughts and the controversy of Affirmative Action is looked at in "The Lie Detector." Lionel goes to a job interview and is told he must take a lie detector test to verify what he has put on his application. Lionel refuses because he sees this as an intrusion on his right to privacy and walks out of the interview. George cannot believe Lionel gave up a chance to have an $18,000 a year job.

Later, the Personnel Director of the company, Mr. Hoffman, comes by to convince Lionel to change his mind. It is suggested that he only wants Lionel back so he can meet the company's obligation to hire a Black person, and to save his own job. However, Mr. Hoffman says he wants Lionel because he thinks Lionel will make a "damn good engineer." Lionel is hired with no lie detector test.

The success of a show depends highly on audience reaction, whether they laugh out loud or cry with the character or hate the villain. If the audience hates the villain, then the actor playing that part is doing a good job. "The Lie Detector" opened my eyes to Hemsley's acting ability. His ability to be the obsequious parent caused me a great deal of discomfort. I was drawn into the scene as if it were real and that, I believe, is one of the components of *The Jeffersons* longevity.

In coming up with ideas for this series the inclusion of an interracial married couple was used to show the unpleasant aspect of George Jefferson as a bigot. He chose not to like his son's fiancée because in his words she was a "zebra." She had a Black mother and a White father. Berlinda Tolbert, Mike Evans and Damon Evans as the Jenny and Lionel characters were essential to the show becoming a hit. At the writing of this book, it is possible to join a Jeffersons group on the internet and see or share pictures of each of them. Judging by the comments that are posted, these actors are almost seen as family. In "The Agreement" Lionel and Jenny are engaged and preparing to marry. George is not happy that his son is marrying a "zebra." Bigotry rears its ugly head, and he tries to get Lionel to have Jenny sign a prenuptial agreement so that when he, George, dies Jenny will not get any of the assets he leaves for Lionel. Lionel blows up, winds up in an argument with Jenny and the wedding is cancelled! When Jenny's father finds her crying her eyes out and discovers that George is the initial cause of her distress, he gets angry and storms out to confront George. In true sitcom fashion, love conquers all. Lionel and Jenny wind up in the elevator together where they kiss and make up and the wedding is back on.

Zara Cully, as Mother Jefferson, perfectly played the role of the comedic idea of a mother-in-law. People related to this idea either as a comedy routine or by having a mother-in-law like Mother Jefferson. After her illness Cully returned to appear in "The Old Flame" episode, funny and irascible as ever. Mother Jefferson invited Harriet Johnson, George's old flame, to dinner at the Jefferson's because she wants to show off his wealth. Lillian Lehman played the part of George's old flame. After the initial opportunity to rehash the old days with his old flame, George gets the unsettling news that she wants to be his "kept woman." When "Weezy" hears this her disbelieving hilarity made me laugh out loud at George as if I was in the room with them.

Lillian Lehman was another talented actor who began her acting career in 1968 in TV shows such as *Julia*, *Ironside*, *The Wild, Wild West*, *Adam-12*, *Sanford and Son*, *The Mod Squad* and *Emergency*! Lehman's acting abilities allowed her to keep working in television every year until 2011, including eleven episodes of *L. A. Law* and eighteen episodes of *General Hospital*. She appeared in the movie *Evan Almighty* (2007), and by 2012 she was an executive producer.

Unfortunately, not everything was coming up roses during this time. On Monday, June 13, 1977, Eric Monte sued Lear, charging him with racial discrimination. Monte claimed that Lear and his production company, T.A.T., violated his civil rights by conspiring to prevent Black writers or producers from marketing prime-time

TV series. In his $250 million suit, Monte alleged that Lear turned over to other writers ideas that Monte originated about Blacks for *Good Times, The Jeffersons,* and *What's Happening.* He claimed that Lear and T.A.T. refused to deal with Black producers and obstructed producers' attempts to deal directly with the networks, per *El Paso Herald Post,* June 14, 1977. According to *Black Enterprise magazine,* June 1978: "Monte alleges he created the Jeffersons, George and Louise (in 1977)". He received a $1 million dollar settlement and a small percentage of the residuals from *Good Times* (which he co-produced). Happily, this suit did not affect the filming of *The Jeffersons.*

Chapter Eight:
Season Four

Episode#62: The Grand Opening, Pt. 1 - September-24, 1977 - Director: Jack Shea - Writer/s: Roger Shulman & John Baskin - Guest/s: Ned Wertimer, Danny Wells, Bill McIntyre, Michael Alldredge, James Staley

George gets overzealous in promoting the opening of his new Corporate Offices and as a result, Louise is kidnapped.

Time Slot Change: September 1977 - March 1978, from Monday 8:00-8:30 to Saturday 9:00-9:30pm -This time slot change decision may have come about since *The Jeffersons* was losing viewers to the TV show *Emergency*.

Episode#63: The Grand Opening, Pt. 2 - September 24, 1977 - Director: Jack Shea - Writer/s: Jay Moriarty & Mike Milligan, Roger Shulman, and John Baskin - Guest/s: Rod Colbin, David Pendleton, Michael Alldredge, James Stale

George's despair turns to anger when it is discovered that the kidnappers made a mistake and took Florence instead of Louise.

Episode#64: Once a Friend - October 1, 1977 - Director: Jack Shea - Writer/s: Michael S. Baser and Kim Weiskopf - Director: Jack Shea - Guest/s: Veronica Redd and Vernon Washington **(See Interview with Michael S. Baser - Chapter Eighteen)**

George gets a double surprise when his old Navy pal unexpectedly shows up and even more unexpectedly has made the change to a woman.

Episode#65: George's Help - October 8, 1977 - Director: Jack Shea - Writer/s: Patt Shea & Jack Shea - Guest/s: Ernest Harden, Jr. (see Episode 60) Mr. Harden's character is now known as Marcus Garvey Henderson, an employee at Jefferson's cleaners. **(See Interview with Ernest Harden, Jr. - Chapter Eighteen)**

George is convinced by Louise to hire a young man recommended by the Neighborhood Help Center; then believes the boy, Marcus, is stealing from the store.

Episode#66: George's Legacy - October 15, 1977 - Director: Jack Shea - Writer/s: Don Segall - Guest/s: Ernest Harden, Jr., Ned Wertimer, F. William Parker, Bhetty Waldron

George has a bust made of himself to leave behind as a legacy, then finds that his real legacy is the people who love him.

Episode#67: Good News, Bad News - October 22, 1977 - Director: Jack Shea - Writer/s: Jay Moriarty & Mike Milligan - Guest/s: Fay Dewitt, Ned Wertimer

Louise gets angry with the Willises when the job she has been expecting, editor of the newsletter for the Neighborhood Help Center, goes to Helen instead.

Episode#68: The Visitors - October 29, 1977 - Director: Jack Shea - Writer/s: Roger Shulman & John Baskin - Guest/s: Jinaki, Hank Rolike

Florence's parents show up at the Jeffersons' apartment and make things unbearable with their constant fighting.

Episode#69: The Camp-Out - November 5, 1977 - Director: Jack Shea - Writer/s: Jay Moriarty & Mike Milligan - Guest/s: Ernest Harden, Jr., Fred Stuthman, Ned Wertimer

George takes Marcus on a camping trip to experience the great outdoors, while "roughing it" they become a little closer.

Episode#70: The Last Leaf - November 12, 1977 - Director: Jack Shea - Writer/s: Laura Levine - Guest/s: No guests - Zara Cully makes her last appearance.

Louise thinks her marriage is in trouble because she has lost her wedding corsage but realizes how much George loves her when he tries to replace the corsage.

Episode#71: Louise's New Interest - November 19, 1977 - Director: Jack Shea - Writer/s: Olga Vallance - Guest/s: Paul Barselou, Percy Rodrigues

Louise almost (unknowingly) becomes romantically involved with the man she works with at the museum.

Episode#72: The Costume Party - November 26, 1977 - Director: Jack Shea - Writer/s: Martin Donovan - Guest/s: Vernon Washington, Priscilla Morrill, Herb Voland

In his effort to win a contract, George turns a pre-costume party cocktail hour into a fiasco.

Episode#73: Florence Gets Lucky - December 3, 1977- Director: Jack Shea - Writer/s: Bob DeVinney - Guest/s: Thalmus Rasulala

A man that George is trying to make a business deal with discovers that Florence is "lucky" for him and takes her on a business trip, which turns out to be unlucky for George.

Episode#74: George Needs Help - December 10, 1977 - Director: Jack Shea - Writer/s: Roger Shulman & John Baskin - Guest/s: Teddy Wilson

Louise and Florence join forces to get George to hire a General Manager for his business

The Jefferson Curve: December 17, 1977 - Director: Jack Shea - Writer/s: Paul M. Belous & Robert Wolterstorff - Guest/s: Ernest Harden, Jr., Ronalda Douglas, Jack Somack

Marcus uses George's "Jefferson Curve" system to get a date.

Episode#76: 984 W. 124th St, Apt. 5C - December 24, 1977 - Director: Jack Shea - Writer/s: Roger Shulman & John Baskin - Guest/s: Ned Wertimer, Alvin Childress, Hope Clarke, Jack Somack, Al White

Louise follows George to a mysterious address in Harlem and makes a surprising discovery.

Episode#77: George and Whitty - January 7, 1978 - Director: Jack Shea - Writer/s: Howard Albrecht & Sol Weinstein - Guest/s: Peter Leeds (as R. S. Whittendale) Ruth Manning, John O'Leary, Mathew Tobin, Ned Wertimer

When George and Louise learn that they are going to lose their apartment, George spends the day trying to become friends with the man he thinks is Whittendale but is really Whittendale's brother.

Episode#78: Lionel Gets the Business (This is Damon Evans last appearance) - January 14, 1978 - Director: Bob Lally - Writer/s: Nancy Vince & Ted Dale - Guest/s: Dwan Smith

When Lionel loses his engineering job, he goes to work for George and almost destroys the Jefferson cleaning business.

Episode#79: The Blackout - January 21, 1978 - Director: Jack Shea - Writer/s: Richard B. Eckhaus - Guest/s: Ernest Harden, Jr., Ned Wertimer, Jack Baker, Bobby F. Ellerbee, Gerald Castillo, Tony Major, Cal Gibson, Tobar Mayo, Ron Trice, Randy Williams, Bill Woodard, La Tari

After a blackout hits New York City, George and Marcus go to the Bronx to check on a store and are arrested as looters.

Episode#80: Florence's Union - January 28, 1978 - Director: Jack Shea - Teleplay by: Andy Guerdat & Steve Kreinberg - Story by: Patt Shea & Jack Shea - Guest/s: Ned Wertimer, Alma Bertrand, William Bogert, Jack Fletcher (as H. L. Whittendale which he plays in six episodes in Seasons 4-11), Bobby F. Ellerbee, Fumilayo, Barbara Mealy, Frances E. Nealy, Dorothy Meyer, Ron Trice, Adrian Ricard, Georgie Paul

When Florence gets involved in a maids' union, George finally meets Whittendale, and it does not go exactly as he always hoped it would.

Episode#81: George and Jimmy - February 4, 1978 - Director: Jack Shea - Writer/s: Richard Freiman - Guest/s: Ned Wertimer, Antony Ponzini, Dave Shelley, Alfie Wise, Bobby F. Ellerbee, Rod Browning

Two FBI agents show up at the Jeffersons' apartment after George makes a "threatening" call to the White House. The situation gets worse when Bentley arrives with a Russian friend from the U. N.

Episode#82: Thomas H. Willis & Co - February 11, 1978 - Director: Jack Shea - Writer/s: Jay Moriarty & Mike Milligan - Guest/s: Ned Wertimer

Helen is happy about Tom starting his own publishing company until she learns that George is the co-signer on the loan.

Episode#83: Uncle George and Aunt Louise - February 18, 1978 - Director: Jack Shea - Writer/s: Roger Shulman & John Baskin - Guest/s: Gary Coleman

George's precocious nephew comes to visit the Jeffersons and brings a lot of tension with him.

Episode#84: George and Louise in a Bind, Pt. 1 - February 25, 1978 - Director: Jack Shea - Writer/s: Jim Rogers - Guest/s: Phillip Charles MacKenzie, Carroll O'Connor, Jean Stapleton

Episode#85: George and Louise in a Bind, Pt. 2 - February 25, 1978 - Director: Jack Shea - Writer/s: Jim Rogers - Guest/s: Phillip Charles MacKenzie

Episode#86: George and Louise in a Bind, Pt. 3 - February 25, 1978 - Director: Jack Shea - Writer/s: Jim Rogers - Guest/s: Phillip Charles MacKenzie

In this retrospective 90-minute show George and Louise are tied up as a burglar loots their apartment. While they are tied up, they remember special moments in their lives.

Episode#87: Jenny's Thesis - March 4, 1978 - Director: Jack Shea - Writer/s: Paul M. Belous & Robert Wolterstorff - Guest/s: Ernest Harden, Jr., Ned Wertimer, Anthony Thompkins, Bob Harcum, Bobby F. Ellerbee, Joseph Burns, Bhetty Waldron, Ron Trice

Jenny's pursuit of a subject for her thesis leads her to the ghetto and to some dangerous realizations.

END OF SEASON FOUR EPISODES

During Season Four Marla Gibbs' name now appears by itself on the beginning rolling credits as opposed to appearing in the ending credits as a guest, and the viewers meet Florence's parents. *The Jeffersons* fell out of the top 30, ranking #56 by the end of the fourth season, even though in at least one journalist's opinion the series was "quite well-written." It was thought that the decline in ratings was due to competition from *Starsky and Hutch* on ABC. From September 1977 to December 1977 *Starsky and Hutch* moved to Saturdays, 9:00-9:30 p.m. competing with *The Jeffersons*, which CBS had moved from its Monday time slot at 8:00-8:30 p.m. to Saturday.

I would not be surprised if people were switching channels. After all, who would want to miss Antonio Fargas as Huggy Bear? Fargas was appearing frequently in so-called Blaxploitation movies and had become a major star. David Soul as Hutch and Paul Michael Glaser as Starsky were the handsome daredevil types, with Starsky driving that hot Ford Torino. *Starsky and Hutch* was an exciting show.

Then again, the reason for the slump could, perhaps, have been what another reporter said, that *The Jeffersons* was the most "listless of the Lear shows." But how could that be said of this season? Marla Gibbs had now become a regular and there certainly was no listlessness about Florence Johnston. Her parents certainly were not listless. Add to that the 90-minute special, which George said was "a night to remember" with scenes from episodes of when the Jeffersons lived next door to the Bunkers and sparks fly. Looking back, I would say that "listless" would be the last word to define this season.

The issues that were brought up were attention-getters for a reason. To bring understanding about the differences among humans and maybe to promote a bit of tolerance. Where else to do this than on a television show where you are sure of an audience and where you can provide some laughter at the same time. Take the episode "Once a Friend." This episode was groundbreaking in that it dealt with a Transgender female who had been George's male friend in the Navy. This episode provided shock, confusion, hilarity, and a close-up look at reality. There was nothing listless about it. The actors were exactly right for the parts written for them. Michael S. Baser and Kim Weiskopf wrote this episode. Baser and Weiskopf were nominated for the Writers Guild of America USA WGA Award (TV) for Episodic Comedy. **(See Interview with Michael S. Baser - Chapter Eighteen.**

If a person was looking for some rousing entertainment, they could not go wrong by watching "The Visitors." Dora Johnston, played by Jinaki, and Don Johnston, Hank Rolike, were Florence's parents and they were in the process of divorcing. They both decided, separately, to stay with Florence for a month or so. As might be expected the Johnstons bickered constantly. Unfortunately, they were also very loud. George, who was not happy about them staying in his home, wants them to leave. Louise tries to get George to stay calm, because, after all, they were Florence's parents and should be treated as guests. George thinks otherwise: "A guest is a guest, a relative is a pest." George finally puts his foot down and tells them how foolish they are acting considering how long they had been married and that they had to get out of his house. Stunned, Dora and Don make up. After which, they tell George they have decided to spend their second honeymoon at the Jeffersons.

It never occurred to me over the years as I watched *The Jeffersons* that Florence had parents. I probably missed that episode. I only discovered this fact while writing this book. The lady who played Florence's mother, Jinaki, had appeared in quite a few TV series and four TV movies from 1976 through 1993. Hank Rolike, playing Florence's father, had also performed in many TV series and five TV movies. His career stretched from 1973 to 1991. The two together were quite overwhelming.

In "George's Help" Ernest Harden, Jr. as Marcus Garvey Henderson, was hired on as George's new employee at Jefferson Cleaners. Marcus steals a jacket on his first day and when George finds out, Marcus gets a stern lecture on morals and how his life could wind up if he chooses to be a swindler. The show's ratings improved after Harden's character was added to the show.

I wondered why Harden's character's middle name Garvey was chosen. Was it in memory of Marcus Garvey who was born in Jamaica in 1887 and who created the "Back to Africa" movement in 1916? Garvey became a well-known public speaker and an inspirational figure for the civil rights era. The fact that the Jeffersons had moved up to the good life in an apartment with White neighbors could have provided a nod to the Fair Housing Act of 1968, which was the so-called ending of the civil rights era.

We learn that George himself is not above shady business dealings when he teaches Marcus about "The Jefferson Curve." In George's words: "I just throw 'em whatever I want them to know." Using a play on words George leads a possible big customer to consider signing a contract with him. He tells Marcus that it is not shady, it's the Jefferson Curve. Marcus is impressed and when a good-looking "fine fox," Natalie Parker, played by Ronalda Douglas, comes into Jeffersons Cleaners he applies George's lesson. After learning she lives in a penthouse and goes to a private school, Marcus gives the young lady the impression that he is the son of the owner of the cleaning establishment.

Of course, she meets George when she picks up her cleaning and tells him she has been dating his son. He thinks it is Lionel. Is

Lionel cheating on Jenny? The misunderstanding leads to the conclusion that Lionel is fooling around, and Jenny knows about it. Tears and recriminations occur back at the apartment. George and Tom argue about who is to blame. During this Jenny stops in and a bit later Natalie drops in hoping to catch Lionel (Marcus). Louise hides the date in the bathroom, Jenny comes out of the kitchen and just as she is about to be told about "the other woman," the real Lionel comes home early. Natalie pops out of the bathroom and chaos ensues. Naturally, Marcus shows up looking for Natalie who was supposed to meet him downstairs. Marcus must admit his lies and blames it on the Jefferson Curve. But all's well that ends well, the confusion is corrected, and Natalie still agrees to go on the date. In the words of Marcus Henderson, well *allllright*!

I cannot say this enough. *The Jeffersons* provided viewers with real-life scenes that would strike a chord, in which they used seasoned, talented actors to portray the realism. A wonderful, heartwarming episode was "984 W. 124th Street, Apt. 5c." Louise follows George one evening believing he is going to see another woman. She discovers that George has been secretly leaving presents at the door of a poor family in an apartment that was once where George lived. The writers of this episode, John Baskin, and Roger Shulman, shared a nomination for the Humanitas Prize for 30 Minute Network or Syndicated Television Award for 1978.

"George and Louise in a Bind" finds them tied up by a thief ransacking the kitchen. The special features are scenes from episodes when the Jeffersons lived next door to the Bunkers. Yes, this special includes yelling and racial slurs, but I know for a fact that if a burglar were in, say my home, during those times, and possibly today, there is no telling what kind of language or objects would be thrown around. (This happened in my house when I was about 8 years old. We were watching television with the lights off and someone came in through the back door. My stepdad hollered at the person and threw a water jug and hit him!) This episode also provided a good example of the various writers' gifts. A slightly different version of the theme song was used at the end.

A damper was placed on the season with the sad news that Zara Cully had become ill again and died at the Cedars-Sinai Medical

Center in Los Angeles on February 28, 1978, from lung cancer. Services were held on March 2, 1978, at the Church of Christian Fellowship, in Los Angeles, California. She was interred at Forest Lawn Memorial Park (Glendale) in the Freedom Mausoleum, Columbarium of Victory. In attendance were the cast and crew of *The Jeffersons*, including show producer Norman Lear. Zara Cully was posthumously awarded an NAACP special Image Award on June 9, 1978, at the 11th Annual NAACP Awards ceremony.

The last episode of the season "Jenny's Thesis" delves into neighborhood gangs, not necessarily a topic for a "situation comedy," but it was a situation that would resonate with viewers. It worked as a thesis for Jenny's school project. Jenny wants to get firsthand information on local gangs, so Marcus takes her to Harlem where a gang called The Black Widows hang out. Despite the implied danger, this episode had the best laugh line, in my opinion. Tom and Helen Willis are in the Jefferson's living room and when Florence mentions that Jenny has gone to see The Black Widows, Tom asks: "Who are the Black Widows, a senior citizens group?" Considering this question came from a White man and the show was aired during the 70s I would say that the line itself was a perfect fit, and it was funny because it was so ridiculous. When Tom and George realize the danger Jenny might be in, the two of them go to Harlem. In the end the viewers get a wake-up call that, unfortunately, gang life can be tragic, even for 12-year-olds.

During the summer hiatus of 1978, Gibbs fans must have been thrilled. In March she was the celebrity hostess for the Annual Ten Best Dressed Women's Affair in Milwaukee; she headlined a parade devoted to all the household workers of America and received the Committee's Woman of the Year Award. The Committee agreed to make the actress's Marla Gibbs Doll their symbolic mascot and pledged to buy thousands of said dolls to pass out to their members.

Gibbs had become popular everywhere, all the time. Gibbs and arranger-conductor Horace Tapscott visited two high schools during this time. At Wilson High School, they spoke to gifted minority sixth-grade students on acting and music careers, they then had lunch with the Home Economics class at Franklin Junior High and spoke to the combined musical and theater arts classes. Gibbs also flew to Texas to serve as celebrity host for the annual telethon sponsored by Paul Quinn College for UNCF (United Negro College Fund). Her popularity even resulted in a national Marla Gibbs Fan Club.

Gibbs knew the show was a success. She sums up the success of *The Jeffersons* well in this article, though she is discussing her character Florence: Florence was a combination of Gibbs' grandmother and an aunt in Chicago. Florence was quoted as saying: "She's like the people I grew up with. You'll find one in every black church. You'll find a Florence all over." "People will walk up to me and say, 'Chile, you're a mess.' They'll do the whole dialogue." "Most Blacks identify with the expressions immediately; it doesn't matter whether it's Chicago or Philadelphia. Most heard their grandmothers say the same things." Gibbs was concerned at the start that the younger viewers could not relate to her. "Then I realized she's in every Black household and that many Whites know someone just like her." *Louisiana Daily Star*.

Florence was a true to life character, and Gibbs liked the role. From a quote in JET Magazine: "I don't think there's any other role I would have liked to have as my initial role to gain recognition. I've been able to get across that each person is important, no matter what their station in life."

Chapter Nine:
Season Five

Episode#88: Louise's Painting - September 20, 1978 - Director: Jack Shea - Writer/s: Nancy Vince & Ted Dale - Guest/s: Robert Doolittle, Ingrid Greer, Sara Seeger

Louise joins an art class and George becomes outraged when he sees her sketch of a male model.

Episode#89: The Homecoming, Pt. 1 - September 27, 1978 - Director: Jack Shea - Writer/s: Jay Moriarty & Mike Milligan - Guest/s: No guests

While Louise worries over a Help Center rent increase and George looks for a cleaning plant, Tom Willis learns that the warehouse he expected to inherit from his father has instead gone to his returned son, Allan (played by Jay Hammer in eight episodes).

Episode#90: The Homecoming, Pt. 2 - October 4, 1978 - Director: Jack Shea -Teleplay by: Paul M. Belous & Robert Wolterstorff and Jay Moriarty & Mike Milligan - Story by: Jay Moriarty & Mike Milligan - Guest/s: T. K. Carter, Gordon Connell, Margaret Wheeler

George connives to get the warehouse; then is surprised to learn that Allan sold it to the Help Center and is not only staying in New York but moving in with the Jeffersons.

Episode#91: How Slowly They Forget - October 11, 1978 - Director: Jack Shea - Story by: Erwin Washington - Teleplay by: Nancy Vince & Ted Dale - Guest/s: Ted Ross and Danny Wells

George looks up an old Navy pal who can get the Help Center's health permit and opens an old wound.

Episode#92: George's Dream - October 18, 1978 - Director: Jack Shea - Writer/s: Bob Baublitz - Guest/s: Candy Mobley, Vernon Washington, James A. Watson, Ned Wertimer

An overworked George dozes off at the office and dreams about life twenty years in the future.

Episode#93: George's New Stockbroker - November 1, 1978 - Director: Jack Shea - Story by: Jim Rogers - Teleplay by Bryan Joseph and Jay Moriarty & Mike Milligan - Guest/s: Jack Knight, Willie Tyler and Lester **(See Interview with Willie Tyler - Chapter Eighteen)**

George is dismayed to learn that his new stockbroker (who is a ventriloquist) was a patient in a mental hospital.

Episode#94: Me and Billy Dee - November 4, 1978 - Director: Jack Shea - Teleplay by: Bryan Joseph - Story by: Jay Moriarty & Mike Milligan - Guest/s: Billy Dee Williams, Ned Wertimer

When Billy Dee Williams visits the Jeffersons' apartment, Florence doesn't believe he is the real thing.

Episode#95: Half a Brother - November 8, 1978 - Director: Jack Shea - Writer/s: Bob Baublitz - Guest/s: Edward Grover, Sally Hightower

George thinks his potential board membership at his bank is in danger when Allan starts dating the daughter of one of the Board Members.

Episode#96: What Are Friends For? - November 22, 1978 - Director: Jack Shea - Story by: Skip Usen - Teleplay by: Jay Moriarty & Mike Milligan - Guest/s: Lloyd Hollar

George's cousin needs a kidney, and George can't decide whether to donate his own.

Episode#97: George Who? - November 29, 1978 - Director: Jack Shea - Writer/s: Christine Houston - Guest/s: Vernon Washington, Herb Davis, Joe Petrullo

George restages his and Louise's first date in an attempt to bring her out of her amnesia.

Episode#98: Harry's Houseguest - December 13, 1978 - Director: Jack Shea - Writer/s: Fred S. Fox & Seaman Jacobs - Guest/s: Carol Swarbrick, Danny Wells

Bentley finds himself engaged to a visitor from England and George tries to help him get rid of her.

Episode#99: George Finds a Father - December 20, 1978 - Jack Shea -Story by: Kurt Taylor & John Donley - Teleplay by: Paul M. Belous & Robert Wolterstorff and Kurt Taylor & John Donley - Guest/s: Arnold Johnson, Raymond Allen

At Christmas time, George invites "Uncle Buddy" over then learns that Buddy was closer to the family than he thought.

Time Slot Change: January 1979 - March 1979, from Saturday 9:00-9:30pm to Wednesday 9:30-10:00pm

Episode#100: Louise's Sister - January 3, 1979 - Director: Jack Shea - Writer/s: Bob Baublitz - Guest/s: Josephine Premice, Justin Lord

Louise's sister, Maxine, visits after thirty years and Louise's bitterness melts when she meets Maxine's son.

Episode#101: Louise's Reunion - January 10, 1979 - Director: Jack Shea - Writer/s: Howard Albrecht & Sol Weinstein - Guest/s: Edye Byrde, Ned Wertimer, Ernie Wainwright

Louise and George attend Louise's high school reunion, and they both learn the truth about Louise's old flame.

Episode#102: A Bedtime Story - January 24, 1979 - Director: Jack Shea - Writer/s: Stephen Neigher - Guest/s: Barrie Youngfellow, Ned Wertimer

George is worried about his sex life (or lack of it) and consults a psychiatrist.

Episode#103: Florence Meets Mr. Right - January 31, 1979 - Director: Jack Shea - Writer: Peter Casey & David Lee - Guest/s: Tamu Blackwell and Larry McCormick. Happily, I was able to speak with one of the writers, David Lee for this and many other episodes. **(See Interview with David Lee - Chapter Eighteen)**

Florence plans to marry a man she has known for three weeks, then realizes he's too ideal.

Episode#104: Louise's Award - February 7, 1979 - Director: Jack Shea - Writer/s: M. Martez Thomas - Guest/s: Sip Culler, Tom Brown, Edmund Stoiber, John Bottoms

George attempts to increase Louise's chance of winning the Help Center's Volunteer of the Year Award by making a large political contribution.

Episode#105: The Other Woman - February 21, 1979 - Director: Jack Shea - Story by: Jack Shea - Teleplay by: Jerry Perzigian & Donald L. Seigel - Guest/s: Judy Landers, Jack Manning, Darlene Conley

Tom is talked into escorting his employer's mistress to a convention in Mexico.

Episode#106: The Hold Out - February 28, 1979 - Director: Jack Shea - Story by: Barnard Mack - Teleplay by: Bryan Joseph - Guest/s: Maxine Elliott Hicks, Vernon Washington, Alma Beltran, E. M. Margolese, Gerald Castillo, Davis Roberts, Robert Phelan, James Ray, Dick Wittington, Peter Turgeon

George refuses to sell his Queens store to a large conglomerate to raise the price.

Time Slot Change: March 1979 - June 1979 from Wednesday 9:30-10:00pm to Wednesday 8:00-8:30pm

Episode#107: The Ones You Love - March 7, 1979 - Director: Jack Shea - Writer/s: Stephen Neigher - Guest/s: Ernest Harden, Jr., David Downing

Florence substitutes for Louise during a magazine interview after Louise and George fight.

Episode#108: Every Night Fever - March 28, 1979 - Director: Jack Shea - Writer/s: Bryan Joseph - Guest/s: Emory Bass

George goes disco, and Louise cannot get him out of it until she takes the lead role in the Help Center play.

Episode#109: Three Faces of Florence - April 4, 1979 - Director: Jack Shea - Story by: Bernard Mack - Teleplay by: Paul M. Belous & Robert Wolterstorff - Guest/s: Jane Brody, Adam Wade

The new Help Center psychiatrist is led to believe that Florence has a split personality.

Episode#110: Louise's Convention - April 11, 1979 - Director: Jack Shea - Writer/s: Paul M. Belous & Robert Wolterstorff - Jay Hammer makes his final appearance as Allan Willis - Guest/s: Sheryl Lee Ralph, Sam MacMurray

Helen and Louise want to go to Los Angeles for the Help Center Convention, and George puts up a fight because it is their anniversary, then decides he wants Louise to go when he makes business plans of his own.

Episode#111: The Freeze-In - April 18, 1979 - Director: Jack Shea - Story by: Jay Moriarty & Mike Milligan - Teleplay by: Jay Moriarty & Mike Milligan and Jerry Perzigian & Donald L. Seigel - Guest/s: Ned Wertimer

The heat goes out in the Willises' and Bentley's apartments, and they spend the night with the Jeffersons, which fouls up George's plan to surprise Louise by remembering the anniversary of their first date.

END OF SEASON FIVE EPISODES

The Jeffersons ranked #49 this season down from #56. Quite possibly because of adding the character Marcus, played by Ernest Harden, Jr., however, it was now in competition with the TV sitcom "*Eight is Enough.*"

Season Five encompasses a myriad of subjects. Societal prejudice, sexism, silliness, trust, adultery, forgiveness, and mental illness, just to name a few. What I took from speaking with Lear is that he knew that these issues would be familiar to every family and so would interest viewers, and that by including laughter in these human experiences provides a sense of hope.

However, some viewers were concerned that the program was not more realistic about being Black in a White world and what cultural barriers this might bring about. Isabel Sanford did not care for the criticisms that *The Jeffersons* was not Black enough. She said, "We're not trying to show the Black experience. We're trying to show day-to-day life. We're not poor, we don't live in the ghetto. We have a mixture of friends, and we have problems like everyone else." Sanford thought one reason for the show's appeal, though, was its universal humor: "We use the mundane things that happen to people, whether they're French or Chinese or what. It's human nature. Everybody can appreciate our humor. There are hotheaded Swedes and hotheaded Japanese, just like George. People love to see George jump up and down and scream."

Roxie Roker was happy with the show. In an interview with Bob Wisehart of the *Knight News Wire*, Roker stated, "We're the only show on the air that has a Black man as head of the household. The family is all together. They've achieved economic success. Within comic restrictions, it isn't such a bad role model."

Societal prejudice is looked at in "The Homecoming," Pts. 1 & 2, and I have to say that the writers did a tremendous job on this episode. Tom and Helen's son, Allan, looks White as opposed to looking like he is mixed-race. George called him a "half-way honky." During this episode George makes Black and White jokes that are not funny to anyone except himself. The audience is treated to a bit of father and son rivalry between Allan and Tom, and Louise is hilarious at mimicking George's cockiness.

Whether anyone realized this at the time, this episode would still be relevant today. Black and White marriages that produce offspring are topics of major concern. This sitcom was on point then and ahead of its time. The staff writers were seasoned well-informed professionals who were not afraid to tackle sensitive issues.

Another way *The Jeffersons* offered comedy was using what was funny in the 1930s. *The Jeffersons* writers would inject this type of comedy here and there. In "How Slowly They Forget" Cornelius X. Mayflower (played by Ted Ross) is the city executive in charge of Building Health Permits and one of George's old Navy buddies. Louise has a week to get a new permit for the Help Center building. This normally takes four weeks. George sets out to Mayflower's office hoping to get the permit right away. While in the office with Mayflower, the two begin to reminisce:

George: The only letters you got was from dum dum Doris. Whatever happened to that loser?

Cornelius: I married her.

They start talking about the practical jokes they played on others while serving on their ship. George confesses to Mayflower that he was the one who put a wig and a dress in Mayflower's old locker. Mayflower is stunned, because during an inspection these items were found, and Mayflower wound up losing a promotion because the ship psychiatrist thought he liked to wear women's clothes. Mayflower had given George the permit, but after hearing what

George did, he takes it back, tears it up and tells George, "It will be a safe night in Central Park before she ever gets a permit from this office!" George finds it difficult to tell Louise he did not get the permit. He goes to the bar downstairs and while he is gone Mayflower shows up at the apartment to apologize. George and Cornelius wind up squaring off when George returns but cooler minds prevail and the two let bygones be bygones and reinforce their close friendship as Navy buddies.

Viewers of *The Jeffersons* got a real treat watching the talented Ted Ross as Mayflower. If they were giving Tony Awards out for sitcoms, he deserved one. Theodore Ross Roberts, also known as Ted Ross, appeared in the 1970 Broadway play *Purlie*, and a 1971 Broadway production of *Raisin*. He was presented with a Tony Award for his role as the Lion in 1975 Broadway production of *The Wiz*.

Situation comedies are meant to entertain. It was Lear's idea of using a myriad of life events, including those that might seem unfortunate, and mixing them with laughter that proved to attract viewers to *The Jeffersons*. The subject of mental illness is explored in "George's New Stockbroker." *Tarrytown NY Daily News* 1978: "George's stockbroker is a ventriloquist, but is he a dummy? Only Louise knows the answer to that one." A real dummy adds to this comedy. Thanks to Willie Tyler and Lester, the show is hilarious.

In "George's New Stockbroker" George hires Ray Crandall (played by comedian and ventriloquist Willie Tyler) unaware of the fact that Ray had recently been in a mental institution. When Ray comes to the apartment he brings his dummy, Lester, with him. Thanks to exclamations from an unaware Florence, the episode is funny; however, it turns out that her remarks are insulting. Remarks like "he sure is crazy!" The message here was that mental illness did not stop people from having a viable career.

Now about Billy Dee Williams. I discovered Billy Dee Williams while watching a movie at a drive-in theater. Judging by the exclamations from the women at that drive-in, I was not the only one that was impressed. In *The Nutty Professor II* (2000), it was still all about Billy Dee, and he is still going strong today as a favorite in the *Star Wars* movies.

In "Me and Billy Dee" Florence is a true Billy Dee Williams fan (Billy Dee from head to toe is hanging on the wall in her bedroom). George, pretending to be Alex Haley, calls Billy Dee and invites him to the apartment for a business meeting. Florence thinks the man who knocks on the door is a Billy Dee Williams lookalike and answers the door in rollers and a house robe. While Williams is in discussion with George, Florence makes it her business to be as rude as possible to the "imposter." Williams informs George that he knows he had not been talking to Alex Haley when George called him. This leads to Florence finding out she is in the same room with the real Billy Dee Williams. (Gibbs facial expressions do not need words.) As he exits the apartment, he cups her face in his hands and kisses her lightly on the lips. "Ciao Bella," he says. I bet a few ladies watched this episode more than once.

This season the Tom and Helen Willis characters were expanded. Roker was incredibly pleased with the change, because she felt the previous seasons' character roles were "appendages to the Jeffersons." She saw the expanded role of the Willis's as an opportunity to bring new elements to the show.

In "The Other Woman" chauvinism and cheating were the order of the day. Thinking Tom is being chauvinistic towards her, Helen declines to travel to Acapulco on a business trip with him. Tom's boss decides to send a secretary in Helen's place. The gorgeous young woman chosen to go on the business trip with Tom, Judy Smith, played by Judy Landers, is seen at the airport by Helen who had decided to go on the business trip after all. As you might imagine, Judy Smith is a real bombshell, and Tom winds up in a real dilemma.

In an interview with Jerry Buck of *The Lowell Sun*, Roker said, "I think what Franklin and I bring to the roles are humanness and naturalness. Many people think Franklin and I really are married." The fact that Roker was, in real life, married to a White man probably helped her and Cover nail their parts.

Chapter Ten:
Photo Section

All in the Family *Cast Sally Struthers, Carroll O'Connor, Jean Stapleton, Rob Reiner, Mike Evans (1971)*

All in the Family Carroll O'Connor, Sherman Hemsley

The Jeffersons Cast Members Roxie Roker, Isabel Sanford, Mike Evans, Berlinda Tolbert, Franklin Cover, Paul Benedict, Sherman Hemsley, Marla Gibbs, Ned Wertimer

The Jeffersons *Isabel Sanford, Sherman Hemsley, Mike Evans (1975)*

The Jeffersons *Cast Members Paul Benedict, Isabel Sanford, Sherman Hemsley, Zara Cully, Franklin Cover, Roxie Roker, Berlinda Tolbert, Damon Evans*

George and Weezy

The Jeffersons episode A Dinner for Harry – Paul Benedict, Roxie Roker, Franklin Cover, Zara Cully

Marla Gibbs as Florence Johnston of The Jeffersons

Ja'net DuBois, Composer of The Jeffersons *theme song Movin' On Up*

The kiss from The Jeffersons *episode "A Friend in Need" - Roxie Roker, Franklin Cover (1975)*

"George's New Stockbroker" - Marla Gibbs, Sherman Hemsley, Lester, Willie Tyler (Photo courtesy Larry Watson)

Celebration of The Jeffersons 200th episode, "The Good Life" - Sherman Hemsley, Norman Lear, Isabel Sanford (Copyright 1983 Embassy Television)

"Me and Mr. G" - Sherman Hemsley, Isabel Sanford, Arlene Wilson

The Jeffersons *Cast with Ernest Harden, Jr. who was cast in two roles as Jason and as Marcus Garvey Henderson (sitting, right)*

Adella Farmar, Costume Designer for The Jeffersons *for 72 episodes, and for Esther Rolle*

Gordon "Whitey" Mitchell

Michael Ross

Rita Riggs, The Jeffersons *Costumer Designer, 2003 Career Achievement Award Winner from the Costume Designers Guild*

The Bobs – Schiller and Weiskoph

Ted Ross as Cornelius X. Mayflower in The Jeffersons *episode "How Slowly They Forget" (1978)*

Zara Cully, Lillian Randolph, veteran of Radio, Film and Television, as Aunt Emma in "Mother Jefferson's Birthday", Isabel Sanford, Sherman Hemsley (1976)

Isabel Sanford, Franklin Cover as Mr. Starch, Sherman Hemsley (1985)

The Jeffersons Cast and Crew (1981). Possibly taken when Marla Gibbs was starring in a spin-off after which she did return to The Jeffersons

Chapter Eleven:
Season Six

Time Slot Change: June 1979 - September 1982, from Wednesday 8:00-8:30pm to Sunday 9:30-10:00pm (this time slot remained the same for three years)

Episode#112: The Announcement - September 23, 1979 - Mike Evans returns - Director: Bob Lally - Writer/s: Jay Moriarty & Mike Milligan - Guest/s: Al Stellone, Henry Sutton

Lionel and Jenny try to keep her pregnancy a secret from George, fearing he will make too many tasteless "zebra" jokes.

Episode#113: A Short Story - September 30, 1979 - Director: Bob Lally - Writer/s: Neil Lebowitz - Guest/s: Matthew (Stymie) Beard, Joe Alfasa, Peter Mitchell, Jesse Jacobs, Bob Gorman, Dave Nicholson, Don Potter, Herbie Tepper

George's glory in receiving an award from The Small Businessmen's Association is short-lived when he discovers the award is given for achievement by a businessman who is five-six and under.

Episode#114: Louise's Old Boyfriend - October 7, 1979 - Director: Bob Lally - Writer/s: Jerry Perzigian & Donald L. Seigel - Guest/s: Richard Shepard, Caleb Chung, Ford Lile, Albert Marotta, Gary Schwartz

When Louise decides not to meet her old boyfriend for dinner, Florence substitutes for her.

Episode#115: Now You See It, Now You Don't, Pt. 1 - October 21, 1979 - Director: Bob Lally - Teleplay by: Mary-David Sheiner & Sheila Judis Weisberg - Story by: Susan Straughn Harris - Guest/s: Danny Wells, James Calvert, Patrick Collins, Bill Calvert, Timothy Gibbs, Charles Walker

As everyone prepares for Charley's Halloween costume party, Louise believes she sees a murder committed in a neighboring building.

Episode#116: Now You See It, Now You Don't, Pt. 2 - October 28, 1979 - Director: Bob Lally - Teleplay by: Peter Casey & David Lee - Story by: Susan Straughn Harris - Guest/s: Charles Walker, Neal Sutton, Patrick Collings, Mimi Cozens, Billy Stevenson

Discovering that Louise is a witness, the killer tries to knock her off.

Episode#117: Where's Papa? - November 4, 1979 - Director: Bob Lally - Writer/s: Peter Casey & David Lee - Guest/s: Danny Wells, Alvin Stanley, Gordon Connell

George decides to have his father's grave moved next to his mother's and gets upset when his father's grave can't be located.

Episode#118: The Expectant Father - November 11, 1979 - Director: Bob Lally - Writer/s: Michael G. Moye **(See Interview with Michael G. Moye - Chapter Eighteen)** - Guest/s: Danny Wells and Earl Bowen

With Lionel's upcoming obligations as a father weighing him down, he and George set out to recapture Lionel's lost youth.

Episode#119: Joltin' George - November 18, 1979 - Director: Bob Lally - Writer/s: Jerry Perzigian & Donald L. Seigel - Guest/s: Ernest Harden, Jr., Luis Avalos, Vernon Washington

George visits a gym with Marcus, mouths off, and ends up in the ring with a boxer.

Episode#120: Baby Love - December 2, 1979 - Director: Bob Lally - Writer/s: Joanne Pagliaro - Guest/s: Roger Robinson, Gino Conforti, Bill Phillips Murry

Florence, upset that everyone but her is married and has children, resorts to trying a video dating service in order to secure a husband.

Episode#121: Louise vs. Florence - December 9, 1979 - Director: Bob Lally - Teleplay by: Jerry Perzigian and Donald L. Seigel - Story by: Paul M. Belous & Robert Wolterstorff, - Guest/s: Dorothy Butts, Fred D. Scott

Florence and Louise fight, disrupting a dinner party George has thrown to impress a high society couple.

Episode#122: Me and Mr. G - December 30, 1979 - Director: Bob Lally - Writer/s: Michael G. Moye - Guest/s: Tom Lawrence, Ailene Wilson, Marlene Warfield

George instructs a young orphan guest in gambling and slang, almost ruining Louise's foster home project.

Episode#123: One Flew Into the Cuckoo's Nest - January 6, 1980 - Director: Bob Lally - Writer/s: Peter Casey & David Lee - Guest/s: Neil Flanagan, Gerry Black, Anthony Gourdine, Kevin Scannell, George Loros, John Tuell, Vernon Weddell

George, making cleaning deliveries to a mental hospital, is mistaken for a patient and finds himself committed.

Episode#124: Louise's Setback - January 13, 1980 - Director: Bob Lally - Writer/s: Robert Wolterstorff - Guest/s: Renee Brown, Dennis Howard, Eve McVeagh, Hank Jones

When a girl Louise counsels at the Help Center attempts suicide, Louise believes it is her fault.

Episode#125: Brother Tom - January 27, 1980 - Director: Bob Lally - Writer/s: Jerry Perzigian & Donald L. Seigel - Guest/s: Starletta DuPois, Dick Anthony Williams

Tom, feeling out of place around Helen's college friends, asks George to teach him how to be Black.

Episode#126: The Arrival, Pt. 1 - February 3, 1980 - Director: Bob Lally - Writer/s: Neil Lebowitz - Guest/s: Lee Bryant, Pat Lawson, Esther Sutherland, Maureen Shannon, Myra Taylor

While Lionel interviews for a job in Boston, George takes Jenny to her Lamaze class. George gets a better education than he expected when Jenny goes into labor.

Episode#127: The Arrival, Pt. 2 - February 10, 1980 - Director: Bob Lally - Writer/s: Michael G. Moye - Guest/s: Don Bovingloh, Brad Blaisdell, Jeanne Campise, Penelope Willis, Ta-Tanisha, Richard Davalos, Pat Lawson, Brion James, Sam DeFazio

When Lionel gets a job in Boston, the Willises and the Jeffersons try to talk him out of it. After the birth of his baby daughter, he decides to keep his family in New York.

Episode#128: The Shower - February 17, 1980 - Director: Bob Lally - Writer/s: Anthony & Celia Bonaduce - Guest/s: No guests

Lionel, feeling the obligation of providing for a family, goes to work on the day of Jessica's baby shower. He returns after George explains that while trying to be a good father, Lionel may miss out on watching his daughter grow up.

Episode#129: The Longest Day - February 24, 1980 - Director: Bob Lally - Writer/s: Bob Baublitz - Guest/s: No guests

While the women go to a fashion show, the men babysit and learn that watching a baby is a full-time job.

Episode#130: George's Birthday - March 2, 1980 - Director: Bob Lally - Writer/s: Jerry Perzigian & Donald L. Seigel - Guest/s: Danny Wells, Ned Wertimer

Upset that no one seems to care about his fiftieth birthday, George's bitterness turns into happiness at his surprise party.

Episode#131: A Night to Remember - March 9, 1980 - Director: Bob Lally - Teleplay by: Peter Casey & David Lee - Story by: Stephen A. Hiller - Guest/s: Renee Jones, F. William Parker, Richard Minchenberg, William McDonald

George's plan to spend his thirtieth wedding anniversary in a hotel suite with Louise is ruined when Louise accuses George of having an affair with his secretary.

Episode#132: The Loan - March 23, 1980 - Director: Bob Lally - Teleplay by: Peter Casey & David Lee - Story by: Anthony Bonaduce & Celia Bonaduce - Guest/s: Irene Dart, Nancy Fox, Arthur Rosenberg, Eddie Quilan

After learning that Lionel's loan for a co-op apartment was turned down, George, Louise, Helen, and Tom all secretly try to secure the loan.

Episode#133: Louise Takes a Stand - March 30, 1980 - Director: Bob Lally - Writer/s: Bryan Joseph and Jerry Perzigian & Donald L. Seigel - Guest/s: William Bogert, Danny Wells

When George decides to take over the lease on Charley's Bar in order to expand his store, Louise exercises her company partnership by refusing to sign contracts.

Episode#134: The First Store - April 6, 1980 - Director: Bob Lally - Writer/s: Jay Moriarty & Mike Milligan - Guest/s: James Keith, Martin Luther King, Jr. (voice only)

George and Louise remember the day George tried to start his own business – an attempt that was altered and shadowed by the assassination of Martin Luther King, Jr.

Episode#135: Once Upon a Time - April 13, 1980 - Director: Bob Lally - Writer/s: Michael G. Moye - Guest/s: David Orr, Walt Hanna, Jeff Seymour, Wendell Wright, Ned Wertimer

George tells baby Jessica a bedtime story, and all is transformed into the fantastic medieval Empire of Jefferson.

END OF SEASON SIX EPISODES

In its sixth season, *The Jeffersons* was one of the top situation comedies; it had returned to the top 10. It remained among the top 20 for the next two seasons.

The show was no longer fodder for the critics. The decision to move the show to Sundays turned out to be gold. This season had something for everyone. There was a bit of slapstick humor, George's bigotry led to serious consequences, and Mike Evans returned and became a father. Suicide is looked at and toward the end of the season there is an emotional return to events of 1968.

Mike Evans returned in "The Announcement." Evans ran into his former co-star, Sherman Hemsley, at the beach and Hemsley suggested that he return to the show. Mike was glad of the fact that he spoke with Hemsley because he may not have returned. He said he would have sooner cut off his hand than to have "gone and asked for the job back." Judging by the ratings for this season, the viewers were also glad.

"The Announcement" elicited the opinion that *The Jeffersons* was sometimes "very back-to-burlesque" or slapstick, and I thoroughly agree. Mr. Withers, the funeral director, is speaking during a memorial for Bentley's bird. Withers introduces Bentley and as he walks up to the podium there is an interruption when a service worker comes through holding the coffin of Sampson the Super Snake, an animal from the circus. They pass right in front of the podium. As the coffin goes by it becomes apparent that it is a very long coffin. As the mourners and Bentley wait for the coffin to pass, they are surprised when a second person comes into view holding the middle, not the end, of the coffin; they continue to wait, and finally the end of the coffin comes into view held by a third worker. I thought this whole scene was funny and very "Laurel and Hardy."

From slapstick to issues like racial injustice was likely one reason *The Jeffersons* remained interesting. Life's deeper issues can be made bearable by using humor. The tone was set for this season for George to make some changes in "Me and Mr. G." Louise brings home a young orphan named Abby for the week. Abby will not talk to anyone at first, but George is able to get her to talk. Unfortunately, George manages to get himself into big trouble by teaching her that a White man is called a honky, and a White woman is called a honkette.

During a visit with a man from the orphanage, Abby calls the man honky. After hearing she learned it from George, Abby is immediately taken back to the orphanage. When George and Louise go to the orphanage to try and make things right, George explains to the little girl that when he was a child, people called him names that hurt him, so he wanted to hurt them back. He admits that it was wrong and apologizes for using the word in front of Abby. As Abby will only speak to George because of her problem as an orphan, the orphanage allows Abby to return to the Jeffersons.

This story focuses on a serious societal issue that does not lend itself well to hilarity. Florence provided a bit of comedy and Jessica's new doll (the doll that pees on people) was kind of funny. This story not only addresses the issue of racism, but it also reminds parents, and grandparents, that they are the people children emulate. For me, the show handled a difficult situation in a believable way.

One would think that a sitcom might not delve too much into certain matters, especially suicide. Today there are many television ads about finding help if one is suicidal, but not so much in the 1970s. *The Jeffersons* was able to share a sense of hope, a desire to help and the reality of trying to be of service. Louise works part-time at the Help Center on the Suicide Helpline. "Louise's Problem" starts out on a good note with a sassy line from Florence. George decides he is not going to work that day. Florence's disrespect for her employer provides a laugh:

Florence: "You mean you stayin' here, all day?"
George: "Yea."
Florence: "Then I ain't!"

Florence decides to go to the Help Center with Louise for the day. The Help Center provides services to the homeless and those in need. Louise gets a chance to appear on a TV program to talk about her work with the Suicide Hotline and she is so excited about it that she forgets she had told a client, Ruthie, to meet her at the Help Center. A distraught Ruthie decides to take her own life by taking a handful of pills. When Louise finds out she is devastated and blames herself. The writers of this episode must have racked their brains to inject some type of humor at this point and they succeeded, barely. George tries to convince Louise that she cannot help everyone. He uses his cleaning business as an example by telling her, "You think I can get out every stain?" Ruthie does not die, and Louise resolves to be more attentive. A difficult subject that *The Jeffersons* was able to present with tact.

Roxie Roker's favorite show of this season was "Brother Tom." Not Brother Tom as in priestly, but Brother Tom as in Black. Tom feels left out when a group of Helen's Black friends show up and they begin talking about old times. Helen's girlfriend mentions how her husband used to look so good in his "velvet sky" (slang for hat). They are having such a good time, Tom decides he needs to fit in because Helen would be happier if he was more like a Black person, so he asks George to teach him how to be Black. Watching Tom trying to be "cool" could not have been funnier. The smooth walk, the hat tilted to the side "Huggy Boy" style, just hilarious. Of course, Tom just did not get it. When he returned to join Helen's friends, he looked absurd, and Helen had to reassure him that she was happy with the man she married. At the end of the lesson George tells Tom to "give me five" and Tom says, "Sure George, you got change for a twenty?"

In the series, Cover's character did not want to be Black; he wanted to understand the Black point of view. Though Tom Willis was fictional, I personally have had White people ask me to help them understand how Black people think. That, in my opinion, is an impossibility. I could say we think heat burns and when it's cold we think we need a jacket like most humans but teaching a White person how to feel and think Black is not doable, in my opinion. But, I have to say that Tom was too cool.

This series endures because it grabs the heart while it tickles the funny bone. It reminds us of our accomplishments and our failures. It shows us love and it shows us hate. In "The First Store" we learned how George tries to get his first store in 1968, the year of the assassination of Dr. Martin Luther King, Jr. Those of us who are old enough may remember how it felt when the reports of King's death were broadcast over television and radio. Those who have learned of it since that time and who have heard his speeches must have some idea of the shock and sadness felt by people around the world. By April of 1980 when this episode aired, *The Jeffersons* was #8 in the ratings. The writers were still on top of their game, and the cast were able to put real feeling into their parts. **(See Chapter Four: The Spin-Off, paragraph 6.)**

Chapter Twelve:
Season Seven

Episode#136:- Marathon Men - November 2, 1980 - Director: Bob Lally - Writer/s: Bob Bendetson & Howard Bendetson - Guest/s: Bob Duggan
Fired up by Helen and Louise's competitive spirit, Tom and George enter the New York Marathon to see who is the more fit.

Episode#137: The Jeffersons Go to Hawaii, Pt. 1- November 9, 1980 - Director: Bob Lally - Writer/s: Michael G. Moye - Guest/s: Wally Amos (Famous Amos), Lincoln Kilpatrick, Sherry Bush
George's doctor tells him he has high blood pressure and should take a vacation and relax. He surprises Louise with a trip to Hawaii and Louise surprises Florence with a ticket to Hawaii.

Episode#138: The Jeffersons Go to Hawaii, Pt. 2 - November 16, 1980 - Director: Bob Lally - Writer/s: Michael Moye and Jay Moriarty & Mike Milligan - Guest/s: Bruce Atkinson, James Grant Benton, Andy Riley, Al Harrington, Richard Sandford
After discovering that Hawaii's relaxed atmosphere keeps his blood pressure down, George contemplates moving there permanently.

Episode#139: The Jeffersons Go to Hawaii, Pt. 3 - November 16, 1980 - Bob Lally - Writer/s: Michael Moye and Jay Moriarty & Mike Milligan, - Guest/s: Fred Ball, William Bryant, Clay Wai, Esmond Chung, Damien Kaha'ulelio, Kimo Kahoano, Krash Keahola
George is eager to invest in some hot Hawaiian property but finds he must enlist Tom Willis's help in convincing Louise to move.

Episode#140: The Jeffersons Go to Hawaii, Pt. 4 - November 23, 1980 - Director: Bob Lally - Writer/s: Michael Moye and Jay Moriarty & Mike Milligan - Guest/s: Fred Ball, Andy Bumatai,

William Bryant, Esmond Chung, Clay Wai, Al Harrington, Douglas Mossman, Moki Palachio, Dr. Stan Carlson

After being washed up on Hawaii's remote North Shore, George and Tom are befriended by a family of Hawaiians who, George later discovers, he will evict if his real estate deal goes through.

Episode#141: Put It On - November 30, 1980 - Director: Bob Lally - Teleplay by: Bob and Howard Bendetson - Story by: Stephanie Haden - Guest/s: Mary Ellen O'Neill, Lee Payne, Donna Blevins, Zan Charisse, Tom Gagen, Geary Douglas

After forbidding their wives to go, Tom and George find themselves on stage in a male strip club.

Episode#142: Florence's Cousin - December 7, 1980 - Director: Bob Lally - Writer/s: Marshall Goldberg - Guest/s: William Allen Young, JoJo De'Amore, Sam Shamshak, J. Christopher Sullivan, Reid Cruickshanks, Ned Wertimer

Florence borrows money from George to lend to her cousin Ernie. When Ernie skips town she is forced to take a part-time job in a greasy spoon to repay the debt.

Episode#143: All I Want for Christmas - December 21, 1980 - Director: Bob Lally - Writer/s: Ron Leavitt & David W. Duclon - Guest/s: Mitzi Hoag, Kaleena Kiff, Sean Garrett McFrazier, Meeno Peluce

George plays Santa Claus at a local orphanage and promises a child a gift he can't deliver: Parents.

Episode#144: Calendar Girl - January 4, 1981 - Director: Bob Lally - Writer/s: David Silverman & Stephen Sustarsic - Guest/s: Susan Krebs, Karen Huie, Annie Gagen

Against Lionel and Jenny's wishes, George and Louise enter Jessica in a baby calendar contest. All is well until the Jeffersons return home with the wrong baby.

Episode#145: As Florence Turns - January 11, 1981 - Director: Bob Lally - Writer/s: Peter Casey & David Lee - Guest/s: No guests

Florence decides to write her own soap opera, but it turns out to look suspiciously like "Dallas."

Episode#146: God Bless Americans - January 18, 1981 - Director: Bob Lally - Writer/s: Peter Casey & David Lee - Guest/s: Jim Weston, Gary Carlos Cervantes

In order to secure an interview on a patriotic talk show, George decides to sponsor a Cuban immigrant.

Episode#147: Alley Oops - January 25, 1981 - Director: Bob Lally - Writer/s: Jerry Perzigian & Donald L. Seigel - Guest/s: Bobby Angelle, Paul B. Price, Michael DeLano, Dorit Stevens

When his best bowler quits the team, George is forced to use Willis in the championship match against Cunningham Cleaners.

Episode#148: And the Doorknobs Shined Like Diamonds - February 1, 1981 - Director: Bob Lally - Writer/s: Michael G. Moye - Guest/s: Ta-Ronce Allen, Vivian Bonnell, Kim Callegari, Sharon Brown, LaShanda Dendy, Carl Lumbly

Hearing that the building she grew up in is about to be torn down, Louise returns to her old apartment and recollects moments of her childhood.

Episode#149: Sorry, Wrong Meeting - February 15, 1981 - Director: Bob Lally - Writer/s: Peter Casey & David Lee - Guest/s: James Karen, Ike Eisenmann

Attending what he thinks is a neighborhood watch meeting, George stumbles into a gathering of the K.K.K. His presence causes their leader to have a heart attack and George must decide whether to administer C.P.R.

Episode#150: My Hero - February 22, 1981 - Director: Bob Lally - Teleplay by: Peter Casey & David Lee and Jerry Perzigian & Donald L. Seigel, - Story by: David Silverman & Stephen Sustarsic - Guest/s: Frances Bay, Jeffrey Clayton, Irwin Keyes, Don Sparks, Leonard Lightfoot, Roger Starks

After saving a woman from a mugging, George is threatened by the lunatic mugger, forcing him to hire a bodyguard.

Episode#151: I Buy the Songs - March 1, 1981 - Director: Bob Lally - Teleplay by: Lesa Kite & Cindy Begal - Story by: Jerry Perzigian & Donald L. Seigel and Peter Casey & David Lee - Guest/s: Danny Wells, Frank De Vol

George tries to write Louise a love song for Valentine's Day after she complains that all he ever does is buy her gifts.

Episode#152: Small Fish, Big Pond - March 8, 1981 - Director: Bob Lally - Writer/s: Michael G. Moye - Guest/s: Jean Byron, Sarah Marshall, David Moses, Tom Williams, Danny Wells

In an effort to solicit business from the really "big boys," George joins a "millionaires" club and winds up accidently donating a hundred grand for their new fountain.

Episode#153: Not So Dearly Beloved - March 15, 1981 - Director: Bob Lally - Teleplay by: David Silverman & Stephen Sustarsic - Story by: Fred S. Fox & Seaman Jacobs, - Guest/s: Lou Rogers III, Earl Billings, Frances E. Nealy, Al Fann, Tracee Lyles, Myrna White, Pucci Jhones, Roy Andrews, Hugh McPhillips

George must deliver a eulogy for a former employee, a man no one, including himself, could stand.

Episode#154: Florence's New Job, Pt. 1 - March 29, 1981 - Director: Bob Lally - Writer/s: Jay Moriarty & Mike Milligan - Guest/s: Larry Linville, Liz Torres, John Anderson

Florence is hired as the head housekeeper of the St. Frederick Hotel.

Episode#155: Florence's New Job, Pt. 2 - March 29, 1981 - Director: Bob Lally - Writer/s: Jay Moriarty & Mike Milligan - Guest/s: Larry Linville, Liz Torres, Ruth Brown, Philip Bruns, John Anderson, Patrick Collins, Sarina C. Grant

Florence faces the problem of firing an employee who has become her friend. (Pilot for episode for *Checking In*)

END OF SEASON SEVEN EPISODES

How this program could combine patriotism, bigotry and comedy is a testament to the writers. The comedy is insulting but funny, as in George telling Florence, "You don't need a beauty nap, you need a beauty coma!" Also, patriotic, and funny, George professes to be a living example of what America is today, and Florence replies, "You sure are, chile, your hair is in recession and your mouth is inflated!"

One thing I noticed in taking this look back is that Florence's role had been expanded. She was finally getting a chance to showcase her overall talent. Florence's quips and sarcastic sense of humor had won her a lot of attention from the television audience, and it could not be denied that the more Florence, the more fun. Mr. Peter J. Boyer would probably have agreed since he stated in the *Lowell Sun*, of Lowell, Massachusetts, that "Gibbs 'Florence' was the best thing about *The Jeffersons*." Not that Florence did not have a presence before this season, she did, but maybe the producers felt it was time to give her a bigger role.

Seems also that someone thought the cast and crew might enjoy a break from the tedium of going to the same studio every day, because in November, cast and crew packed up and went to Hawaii to film, that's right, "The Jeffersons go to Hawaii." While there they were invited to the home of Wally Amos. Viewers were told that George needed to lower his blood pressure (it is mentioned that this is a major problem with Black males), so he decided to take a vacation. Even Florence gets to go on the trip when Louise decides to buy her a ticket.

Other top-rated shows at the time were used for inspiration. For instance, one of the best episodes of the season, in my opinion was "As Florence Turns." Florence writes a soap opera that gives a nod to the popular television series, *Dallas*. George is portrayed as the evil, greedy head of the family, GR. He tries to get Lionel fired from his job as an electrical engineer to force Lionel to come work for him. Watching George's facial expressions as he is trying to keep Louise from sharing this with Lionel is an acting lesson in itself. There were no guests, and none were needed. GR gets shot, but he doesn't die. Florence had written herself into the soap as "Flossie," the maid who GR had fired. Flossie returns (after a date with Billy Dee Williams) as a Mae West-type in a fur coat and diamond earrings and confesses that she shot GR. Flossie has sold her soap opera movie rights and has bought the Whittendale Building and since she had not killed George, she delights in putting him out of the building.

Giving Gibbs more exposure by having her step out of her maid role added interest and enjoyment to *The Jeffersons*. Ideas of doing a spin-off were certainly floating around in someone's head.

If nostalgia was your thing, it could be found here. Louise learns that her old childhood residence is to be torn down. She decides to visit the building at once. In "And the Doorknobs Shined Like

Diamonds" while Louise is in her old bedroom, she has memories of those times when her mother was still alive. She remembers how, as a child she thought her mother favored her older sister and she remembers the talk she had with her mother and finds out her mother loved her and never worried about her getting on in life. The story is beautifully heart-wrenching. "And the Doorknobs Shined Like Diamonds" is one of the only episodes to end without the show's iconic ending theme. The credits instead roll over complete silence.

In "I Buy the Songs," romance, or lack thereof, was the order of the day. George does not have a present for Louise for Valentine's Day. Louise is surprised George does not realize it is Valentine's Day. But George, as usual, pretends otherwise, "Of course I know its Valentine's Day, how can I forget that?" To which Florence replies, "Nobody could blame you if you did, I mean you can't be expected to remember it's Valentine's Day and your way home from work." After they hear Tom reciting a poem to Helen, Louise needs something to show her how special she is to George. George, after trying to give Louise money as a present, must learn that money does not convey the feelings of the heart. He winds up finding someone to write a song for him to sing to her, Sammy the songwriter, played by Frank DeVol. In a touching scene, George gathers everyone into the Whittendale Building's bar, and he sings the song to Weezy. Romance was in the air. Of course, Louise finds out George did not write the song, but through Bentley, who had accompanied George on the piano, Louise is convinced that the song was heartfelt, and Louise and George begin to dance. This episode was so touching even Florence cried. Play it again, Bentley.

The guest, Frank DeVol, actor, arranger, and composer had been nominated for four Academy Awards by the time he appeared on *The Jeffersons*. His career began in 1923. DeVol had worked with Nat King Cole, Ella Fitzgerald, Tony Bennett, Dinah Shore and Doris Day. His most famous arrangement was Nat King Cole's *Nature Boy*. He wrote the television theme tune for *The Brady Bunch*, *My Three Sons* and *Family Affair*. He also appeared in movies and on several television programs. DeVol's character helped make this episode deeply heart-warming.

Black pride pops up in "Florence's New Job, Pt. 2." The message resonated with me due to the old-school type of line from Florence, in reply to a remark from a colleague: "I ain't no neophyte, I'm a church goin' woman!" On the serious side, in answer to a snide remark from a maid at the Hotel, Florence said, "In the Black race I belong to, self-achievement comes way ahead of stealing." Whether that was an ad-lib or a writer's line it spoke to a very deep subject. The writers Jay Moriarty and Mike Milligan were familiar with the old school joke lines and as White writers they had enough insight to be able to connect with the Black actors' feelings which in turn contributed to the reality of the actor's delivery of the lines.

"Florence's New Job" was written as a send-off for Gibbs who had been in talks about a possible spin-off series titled *Checking In*, in which she would star as the Executive Housekeeper for the St. Frederick Hotel. Someone noticed that Gibbs had that stand-alone quality. The show debuted on April 9, 1981. However, the series cancelled after four episodes, ending the show on April 30, 1981. Gibbs returned to *The Jeffersons*. It was explained that the St. Frederick Hotel had burned down, so Florence decided to return to her former job with the Jeffersons. It must have seemed clear, however, that Gibbs was looking at a brighter future in TV land.

A wonderful climax to this season was Isabel Sanford finally winning an Emmy for Outstanding Lead Actress in a Comedy Series. She had been nominated a few times before and was almost used to not winning the Emmy. Sanford was backstage having a snack as opposed to sitting in the audience when the nominations were announced. She was still chewing as she walked to the podium. When Sanford accepted her Emmy at the podium her first words were, "At last." Everyone laughed and applauded. After mentioning the cheese in her mouth (because she was not expecting to win) she then said, "See, I've waited so long, all my humility is just gone!" Along with general thanks to everyone involved with getting her to that moment, she only named two names. She thanked God and she thanked Norman Lear for hiring her. Her acceptance speech was uploaded to YouTube on August 16, 2008, by her son. It is titled: Isabel Sanford gets an Emmy.

Chapter Thirteen:
Season Eight

Episode#156: The Separation, Pt. 1 - October 4, 1981 - Director: Bob Lally - Teleplay by: Bob Bendatson & Howard Bendetson - Story by Jay Moriarty & Mike Milligan - Guest/s: Berlinda Tolbert, Mike Evans

Jenny and Lionel decide to separate and possibly get a divorce. The Jeffersons and Willeses are very upset.

Episode#157: The Separation, Pt. 2 - October 11, 1981 - Director: Bob Lally - Teleplay by: Ted Dale & Nancy Vince - Story by: Jay Moriarty & Mike Milligan - Guest/s: Berlinda Tolbert, Mike Evans, Bob Delegall

Jenny and Lionel talk over their problems, solve them, and get back together. Everyone is happy.

Episode#158: Louise's Father - October 18, 1981 - Director: Bob Lally - Writer/s: Jerry Perzigian & Donald L. Seigel - Guest/s: Leonard Jackson, John Hawker

George spots a picture in the newspaper of a man who he thinks is Louise's father. Louise thinks George is crazy. Her father's been dead for forty years.

Episode#159: My Maid, Your Maid - October 25, 1981 - Director: Bob Lally - Writer/s: Peter Casey & David Lee and Jerry Perzigian & Donald L. Seigel - Guest/s: Roseanna Christiansen, Diana Webster

Unknown to the other, George and Louise each hire a maid. When the two maids report for duty neither George nor Louise sends their maid back. All hell breaks loose. Eventually Louise's maid gets the job.

Episode#160: I've Still Got It - November 1, 1981 - Director: Bob Lally - Writer/s: Fred S. Fox and Seaman Jacobs - Guest/s: Danny Wells, Vernee Watson, Joycelyne Lew, Frank Dent

George wonders if he is losing his sex appeal. His beautiful young secretary, Carol, bolsters his confidence. Louise wonders whether it's proper for George to be basking in Carol's flattery (most of which George imagines himself), then graciously decides it is.

Episode#161: Florence Did It Different, Pt. 1 - November 8, 1981 - Director: Bob Lally - Writer/s: Michael G. Moye - Guest/s: Roseanna Christiansen.

Louise explains to the new maid, Carmen, what made Florence so special. A montage of clips about Florence is used.

Episode#162: Florence Did It Different, Pt 2 - November 15, 1981 - Director: Bob Lally - Writer/s: Michael G. Moye - Guest/s: Roseanna Christiansen

After George and Louise promise Carmen a job, Florence comes back after the St. Frederick Hotel burns down to reclaim her old job, which was also promised to her.

Episode#163: The House That George Built - November 29, 1981 - Director: Bob Lally - Writer/s: Jerry Perzigian & Donald L. Seigel - Guest/s: Rodney Kaygeyama, Phil Rubenstein, Peter Lawford (voice only)

After having a brush with death, George decides to write his autobiography, so when he does die the world will be left with an account of his remarkable life. Realizing that writing is tough work, he instead opens up a museum dedicated to himself.

Episode#164: A Whole Lot of Trouble - December 6, 1981 - Director: Bob Lally - Writer/s: Jerry Perzigian & Donald L. Seigel - Guest/s: No guests

Unknowingly, George buys a piece of property that the Help Center has been using for children's recreation. When Louise discovers this, she begs him to give the land back to the kids. He won't budge. He wants to open a new store. Finally, over a game of basketball, a nine-year-old boy convinces George to do the right thing.

Episode#165: I've Got a Secret - December 20, 1981 - Director: Bob Lally - Writer/s: Jerry Perzigian & Donald L. Seigel and Peter Casey & David Lee - Guest/s: No guests

George finally manages to read Louise's secret diary and is shocked to find that she is having several affairs. Of course, it is a fake diary Louise had planted because she knew George could not resist snooping.

Episode#166: A Charmed Life - December 27, 1981 - Director: Bob Lally - Writer/s: Peter Casey & David Lee - Guest/s: Daniel Frishman

After being left off the invitation list to a swank party, George decides to take charm lessons to ingratiate himself with the upper class.

Episode#167: Thammy the Thongwriter - January 3, 1982 - Director: Bob Lally - Writer/s: David W. Duclon & Ron Leavitt - Guest/s: Frank DeVol, Tom Case, Victoria Jackson

George asks his new songwriting neighbor, Sammy Gelson, to write a jingle for Jefferson Cleaners. Sammy can't because he is heartbroken over his wife leaving him. George takes him to a singles bar in hopes of finding Sammy a new woman and getting his jingle written.

Episode#168: I Spy - January 17, 1982 - Director: Bob Lally - Writer/s: Sara V. Finney - Guest/s: Terry Carter, Edward Penn, Alex Rodine

George suspects Helen of having an affair. Does he or does he not tell Tom? He decides to take Tom to a rendezvous point so Tom can see for himself. Tom learns a valuable lesson about trust.

Episode#169: Dog-Gone - January 24, 1982 - Director: Bob Lally Writer: Mark Rothman & Jeffrey Duteil - Guest/s: Ivor Francis (as H. L. Whittendale) and Olive Dunbar

To get on Mr. Whittendale's good side, George agrees to babysit for the building owner's dog. During a game of toss and fetch George accidentally tosses the ball over the balcony, and the dog follows. George loses any business rapport he had with Whittendale.

Episode#170: Blazing Jeffersons - January 31, 1982 - Director: Bob Lally - Writer/s: Peter Casey & David Lee and Jerry Perzigian & Donald L. Seigel - Guest/s: Logan Ramsey, Don Dolan

A blaze destroys one of George's cleaning stores. The cause: faulty wiring which had been installed by Lionel.

Episode#171: Men of the Cloth - February 7, 1982 - Director: Bob Lally - Writer/s: Michael G. Moye - Guest/s: Andrea Crouch, Esther Sutherland, Myra Taylor, Erin and Leslie Holland, Pat Lawson

George gets Andrae Crouch to sing at Jessica's baptism, after Jenny had promised Florence and her choir group the job.

Episode#172: A Case of Self-Defense - February 21, 1982 - Director: Bob Lally - Writer/s: Joyce Gittlin & Jeffrey Richman - Guest/s: Frank DeVol, Ashley Hester, Rick Podell, Erin and Leslie Holland, Danny Wells

Ignoring Louise's, pleas, George gets a handgun for the apartment only to have a near fatal accident with baby Jessica.

Episode#173: My Wife, I Think I'll Keep Her - March 7, 1982 - Director: Bob Lally - Writer/s: Peter Casey & David Lee - Guest/s: Karrie Emerson

George makes a commercial and Tom publishes a book that their wives object to. Tempers flare and the women leave the men to fend for themselves without the "womenfolk."

Episode#174: Guess Who's Not Coming to Dinner? - March 14, 1982 - Director: Bob Lally - Writer/s: Brian Pollack & Rick Shaw - Guest/s: No Guests

When she is not invited to a party for the Willises' "close friends", Florence drowns her sorrows in George's expensive wine.

Episode#175: The Strays, Pt. 1 - March 21, 1982 - Director: Bob Lally - Writer/s: Michael G. Moye - Guest/s: Lydia Nichole **(See Interview with Lydia Nichole – Chapter Eighteen)**, Leonard Lightfoot, Irwin Keyes, Will Gill, Jr., LaSaundra Hall

George gets Louise's wedding ring remounted for their thirty-third anniversary, only to get it ripped off by a street gang made up of girls.

Episode#176: The Strays, Pt. 2 - March 28, 1982 - Director: Bob Lally - Writer/s: Michael G. Moye - Guest/s: Lydia Nichole, Leonard Lightfoot, Irwin Keyes, Bernadette Colognne, LaSaundra Hall, Joe Rosario

In a desperate attempt to retrieve Louise's wedding ring, George invades the hangout of the street gang only to find himself in even more trouble.

Episode#177: Jeffersons Greatest Hits - April 11, 1982 - Director: Bob Lally - Writer/s: Ralph Phillips - Guest/s: James A. Watson, Jr., Steve Tracy

In an attempt to rescue Florence from the clutches of a couple of crooked record promoters, George gets bamboozled himself: he pays big money to get the guys to record him and make him a star. Florence winds up saving the day.

Episode#178: A Small Victory - April 18, 1982 - Director: Bob Lally - Writer/s: David W. Duclon & Ron Leavitt - Guest/s: Lynne Moody, Greg Zadikov, Peter Schrum

Louise and Helen decide to quit the Help Center when they cannot persuade a young prostitute to leave her pimp after he beat her up. They soon find out, however, that they did get through to her and change their minds about quitting.

Episode#179: Lesson in Love - May 2, 1982 - Director: Bob Lally - Writer/s: Jerry Perzigian & Donald L. Seigel - Guest/s: Kene Holliday, Carl Held

Florence's confidence goes when a date drops her off early. Feeling sorry for her, Louise invites a guy over to meet her and he asks her out. With Louise and George's "help" Florence is almost sorry they tried to help her.

Episode#180: Do Not Forsake Me, Oh My Helen - May 16, 1982 - Director: Bob Lally - Writer/s: Peter Casey & David Lee - Guest/s: Stan Haze, Clyde J. Barrett, James McIntire, Bob Gorman, Andy Jarrell, and Danny Wells

Feeling threatened by the impending return of Helen's old boyfriend, Tom daydreams of how he would handle the situation had it occurred in the old west.

END OF SEASON EIGHT EPISODES

Season Eight debuted at #3. Paul Benedict left the show to pursue other interests. In the beginning credits they added Tom sauntering in being "cool."

Marla Gibbs had become a fan favorite due to her sassy portrayal of Florence. "Where is your backbone, don't they make them in your size?" In "Florence Did It Different, Pt. 1," there were flashbacks of previous episodes; Pt. 2 was all Florence. She wants to have her old job back after the fire at St. Fredericks and does not realize the position has been filled. Florence insults George and he refuses to give her the job back. Since Florence seems to be desperate to get her job back, George decides to re-hire her if she agrees to his terms. But of course, the tables are turned; George asks her to get on her knees and beg, she says, "Forget it Mr. Jefferson." He says, "One knee." She says, "Uh, uh." He says, "Sitting in a chair." She says, "No." He says, "Well, just say please." Florence hesitates. "Well," and George says, "Aw, please Florence, I'll do anything." Florence gets her job back and somehow George thinks he has won.

Staying at the top is not easy. Every member of an audience must be satisfactorily entertained. Death may not normally lend itself as entertainment in a situation comedy, but death is a part of living that cannot be ignored. After George almost drowns in a boating accident, he realizes he does not want to die as a nobody. He wants headlines to read "George Jefferson Dies!" (Florence quips, "I heard that.") George decides that he wants to be remembered as a somebody after he is gone. "The House that George Built" was an excellent episode. George builds a museum dedicated to himself showcasing his life over the years. Pictures highlight his early years as a child, the lean years, and the filthy rich years. Peter Lawford voiced the museum guide. "George Jefferson, a man, a legend, a dude with a lotta bucks." When giving directions to the visitors to the museum, Lawford also repeats the directions in Spanish. This episode shines a light on a much different hidden version of George, a man who just wants to be remembered by someone. Something with which every viewer could identify.

Peter Lawford's voice was very recognizable. He had been in the entertainment business fifty years by the time he voiced the museum guide; he had appeared on radio shows, television and in at least 80 movies. A real treat for *The Jeffersons* viewers.

To keep that winning spot, *The Jeffersons* writers would sometimes use true stories as inspiration. "Dog-Gone" was shocking. It also made me laugh out loud. I could hardly believe the producers allowed it to be shown. I got in touch with the writer, Mark Rothman, and he was good enough to explain to me in an email how he got the idea for this episode: "The idea for that episode came from my recounting the true story of Mike Nichols, the famed director, having experienced that incident, of being in a high-rise building, watching a great Dane, playing catch with him near an open window in the living room of a friend and seeing him sail out the window to his death. When the owners returned, Nichols indicated that the dog seemed "quite depressed". That one line was enough to sell it to the *Jefferson's* producers to recreate that for George Jefferson. They executed it pretty much the way I wrote it."

Marla Gibbs talent now began to be showcased in a bigger way. In "Men of the Cloth" George pretends to be a reverend to finagle a specific preacher (Andrae Crouch) into christening Jenny and Lionel's baby. George rearranges the apartment – he hangs a picture of The Last Supper. He gets a new Bible, telling Louise their old one was 20 years old and "I'm sure a lot of stuff has happened since then!" Crouch discovers George's subterfuge and decides to call George up to say a word at the ceremony. George, of course, rearranges a Bible verse by saying, "It is harder for a rich camel to get into needle heaven." This was so funny even Helen had to give in and laugh at George. In the same scene at the church Florence sang with Crouch! I had no idea that Gibbs could sing. This was wonderful casting.

Andrae Crouch at the time was a songwriter, singer, record producer and pastor. Some referred to him as the "father of modern gospel music." One of Crouch's songs, "The Blood Will Never Lose Its Power" is a standard in churches worldwide.

The Jeffersons producers had a good idea that viewers wanted to see more of Florence. In "Guess Who's Not Coming to Dinner" Marla gets to add a different side to Florence after she and Ralph drink George's $500 bottle of wine, "To all the people who do the dirty jobs for the people who eat prime rib." Gibbs's versatility lent plenty of laughs, along with Ned Wertimer's portrayal of Ralph the doorman, who never disappoints in his ability to get a generous tip and who winds up inside the Jefferson's apartment opening that bottle of wine. Florence gets tipsy believing a party is being given by Louise and George and the Willises to which she has not been invited. After sharing with everyone what she thinks of them, she notices a cake on the table and discovers that the cake was for her surprise birthday party. Watching a drunk Florence had to have been relatable and funny to a few television viewers. This episode may have been a nod to the movie "Guess Who's Coming to Dinner" (1967) in which Sanford played the maid, Tillie Binks.

In the ten years this show was on the air, I am surprised the script never called for Florence to smack George Jefferson upside the head. He laughed at her unmercifully. But George was fond of her and after hearing about her problem catching and keeping a man, he shows her, by play acting, how to be a "sexy woman." Florence insists she is not going to act like a loose woman. In reply to Florence's remark, George says, "I'm not telling you to be a loose woman, all I'm doing is saying loosen up a little bit." George tells her she must be on the offense. Watching him show Florence how to bat her eyes deserved a standing ovation. On her next date Florence takes George's advice, only the consequences are not what she expects, or rather, the consequences were what she originally feared. Between George's advice and the fact that Louise was the one who got the date for Florence - butting in, as it were - Florence begins to feel depressed, that is until she gets a phone call from a former boyfriend and, instantly, all's right with the world again.

By this time in the airing of the series, it appears as if everyone is happy with *The Jeffersons*. There were little or no negative comments by television critics that I could find in my research. The show was funny, even silly at times which is what makes me laugh. It was relatable and a bit off-the-wall. Entering the ninth season it was the longest running show featuring Blacks since the *Amos 'n Andy* television program. Sanford attributed the success to "the chemistry between the actors and the production company." Personally, looking back, I think Marla Gibbs as Florence Johnston contributed a great deal more to the success of *The Jeffersons* than has been noted. She stood out like a beam of light, even when the script called for sadness.

Chapter Fourteen:
Season Nine

Time Slot Change: September 1982 - December 1984, from Sunday 9:30-10:00pm to Sunday 9:00-9:30pm

Episode# 181: Laundry is a Tough Town, Pt. 1 - September 26, 1982 - Director: Bob Lally - Writer/s: Kurt Taylor and Mark Miller - Story by: Elliot Stern - Guest/s: Thomas Calloway, Billy Sands

When a rival cleaning store threatens to run George out of business with their "Millionth Customer" promotion he laughs in their face. But his spirit is broken when Louise accidentally becomes the millionth customer. George decides to retire.

Episode#182: Laundry is a Tough Town, Pt. 2 - October 3, 1982 - Director: Bob Lally - Writer/s: Michael G. Moye and David W. Duclon & Ron Leavitt - Guest/s: Berlinda Tolbert, Thomas Calloway, Ben Frommer

George's retirement drives Florence and Louise crazy until Louise finally convinces George he is still a vibrant man and should go back to work.

Episode#183: Anatomy of a Stain - October 10, 1982 - Director: Bob Lally - Writer/s: Peter Casey & David Lee - Guest's: Earl Montgomery, Dick Gjonola, Randall Nazarian

Tom accuses Jefferson Cleaners of staining his pants. George claims Tom left a candy bar in the pants and is responsible for the stain. For its publicity value, George decides to bring the case to a TV show, a la, *The People's Court*. The show, however, never reaches the air because George interferes with the judge's ruling. Both George and Tom learn that TV court is no place for friends to air their dirty laundry.

Episode#184: Social Insecurity - October 17, 1982 - Director: Bob Lally - Writer/s: Jerry Perzigian & Donald L. Seigel - Guest/s: No guests

When George refuses to discuss a pension plan for her, Florence gets Louise, the Willises and friends to help campaign for her cause. When they actually start to picket him, George reluctantly reveals his "video will" which contains retirement provisions for Florence.

Episode#185: Charlie's Angels - October 24, 1982 - Director: Bob Lally - Writer/s: Neil Lebowitz - Guest/s: Margaret Michaels

Tom puts up the money for Charlie to redo his bar. Using George's idea of waitresses in skimpy angel costumes turns the place into a goldmine, causing George to beg for a piece of the action. The women in the building revolt at the sexist exploitation.

Episode#186: Heeeere's Johnny - October 31, 1982 - Director: Bob Lally - Writer/s: Michael G. Moye - Guest/s: Johnny Brown

Johnny, a loud, obnoxious old friend of George's comes back into the Jefferson's life and stays with them much against Louise's will. When Louise learns Johnny is broke, she goodheartedly suggests Johnny for a job at their cleaning store.

Episode#187: A Date with Danger - November 7, 1982 - Director: Bob Lally - Writer/s: Peter Casey & David Lee - Guest/s: William Marshall, Young Sun, Keone Young

Florence's date with a charming, erudite novelist is interrupted by the Jeffersons and the Willises who fear for her safety because the man is a convicted murderer. The four soon regret their judging the man without knowing that he was convicted of murder for an accidental death under extenuating circumstances. All agree that everyone deserves a second chance.

Episode#188: Death Smiles on a Dry Cleaner, Pt. 1 - November 21, 1982 - Director: Bob Lally - Teleplay by: Jerry Perzigian & Donald L. Seigel - Story by: David Duclon & Ron Leavitt - Guest/s: Barrie Ingham, Bernard Fox, Russell Johnson, David Downing, Edie McClurg, Dorothy Konrad, David Downing, Teresa V. Hoyos, Steve Nevi, Bill Erwin, Zale Kessler, Robert Burleigh

Because of George's passion for mysteries, Louise finagles him onto a mystery writer's cruise during which a made-up mystery is to be solved by the passengers. Accompanying George are Louise and Florence who has a shipboard romance with one of the writers who is murdered. Fun turns into fear when the lives of all aboard are threatened.

Episode#189: Death Smiles on a Dry Cleaner, Pt. 2 - November 28, 1982 - Director: Bob Lally - Teleplay by: Peter Casey & David Lee - Story by: David Duclon & Ron Leavitt - Guest/s: Barrie Ingham, Bernard Fox, Russell Johnson, David Downing, Steve Nevi, Edie McClurg

George is the laughingstock of the ship when he disagrees with everyone's solution of the writer's murder. But he has the last laugh when, deducing that the captain and the duchess are one and the same, he solves the crime, which is actually part of the made-up mystery, and wins the cruise's grand prize.

Episode#190: Appointment in 8-B - December 12, 1982 - Director: Bob Lally - Writer/s: David W. Duclon & Ron Leavitt - Guest/s: Sheila Wills (DeWindt), Grand L. Bush (Grand Bush)

Ralph's eavesdropping leads him to believe that George is having an affair with another woman in the building. When Ralph lets this slip to Louise, she confronts the woman only to find out it was a different George.

Episode#191: Poetic Justice - December 29, 1982 - Director: Bob Lally - Writer/s: Lou Messina & Diane Messina Stanley - Guest/s: Peter White

George is humiliated when everyone in the building reads and adores his old love poems to Louise. But when a poetry publisher friend of Tom's makes an appointment to see him, George thinks he is the next T. S. Eliot and launches a writing spree that results in some pretty obnoxious verse.

Episode#192: How Now Dow Jones - December 26, 1982 - Director: Bob Lally - Writer/s: Peter Casey & David Lee - Guest/s: Bebe Drake (Bebe Drake-Massey), Vanda Barra, Adrian Ricard, Marianne Muellerleile

Florence and her friends get George to invest their money in the stock market. As their money grows so does their admiration for George. His greed for their hero worship clouds his financial judgment and they lose everything. George absorbs the loss.

Episode#193: The Defiant Ones - January 2, 1983 - Director: Bob Lally - Writer/s: Jeffrey Richman & Joyce Gittlin - Guest/s: Rebecca Stanley, Jan Stratton

George hides a photo from Louise by locking it in his office safe. Louise thinks it is a picture of a woman. She and Helen break into the safe and wind up in jail. The photo turns out to be a picture of George's childhood teddy bear.

Episode#194: My Maid, My Wife - January 8, 1983 - Director: Bob Lally - Teleplay by: Marilyn Anderson & Wayne Kline - Story by: Michael Poryes - Guest/s: Kim Hamilton, Ken Olfson

Florence is too embarrassed to tell an extremely rich ex-school chum that she is "just a maid." George and Louise agree to let Florence be Mrs. Jefferson for a day and Louise the maid. The chum is rude to Louise which causes Florence to stop the charade.

Episode#195: Mr. Wonderful - January 16, 1983 - Director: Bob Lally - Writer/s: Jerry Perzigian and Donald L. Seigel - Guest/s: Sandy Helberg

When George lets it slip that Tom has bought life insurance for a cousin Helen hates, the fight that ensues splits the Willises. George intervenes and gets them back together.

Episode#196: My Girl, My Louise - January 23, 1983 - Director: Bob Lally - Writer/s: Sandy Sprung and March Vosburgh - Guest/s: Amzie Strickland

Louise swallows her pride and asks her former employer for a donation for the Help Center. The woman treats Louise like a servant and Louise explodes. Fortunately, the woman is not wearing her hearing aid and decides to tell Louis what a fine person she is. Louise gets the donation.

Episode#197: Bodyguards Are People Too - January 30, 1983 - Director: Bob Lally - Writer/s: Wade Stevens and Brent Stevens - Guest/s: Irwin Keyes

Jenny confesses to the Jeffersons and Willises that she is about to give up fashion design. George's one time bodyguard wants to settle down and picks Jenny at first sight. He later realizes he should wait for Miss Right. His decision influences Jenny and she decides not to give up fashion design.

Episode#198: True Confessions - February 6, 1983 - Director: Bob Lally - Teleplay by: Peter Casey & David Lee - Story by: Lew Goldstein - Guest/s: Garrett Morris, Michael Pataki

George and Louise learn that Jimmy, the foster child they have supported for years, is, in reality, a full-grown man.

Episode#199: Mr. Clean - February 13, 1983 - Director: Bob Lally - Writer/s: Marita Epp & Carole Oleson - Guest/s: Will Gill, Jr., Bobby Herbeck, Dap "Sugar" Willie

George bets Florence he can do all her housework in an afternoon. He and Tom do such a bad job they hire a cleaning crew. George must admit to Florence that her job is harder than it looks.

Episode#200: The Good Life - February 20, 1983 - Director: Bob Lally - Writer/s: Michael G. Moye - Guest/s: Gladys Knight, Pat Lawson, Esther Sutherland, Frankie Albright, Stefan Ross, Melodee Spevack, Susan Plumb, Larry Humburger

When Helen raves about being made over at a celebrity filled, high-priced beauty salon, Florence decides to blow her savings and get a taste of the good life. While in the salon, Florence meets Gladys Knight but does not recognize her under her face mask.

Episode#201: Father's Day - March 6, 1983 - Director: Bob Lally - Teleplay by: Jerry Perzigian & Donald L. Seigel - Story by: Hans Kraucauer - Guest/s: Norman D. Wilson, Dain Turner

After a boy enlists George's participation in a father/son bowling tournament, George learns the boy's father is not dead but physically handicapped. George makes the boy aware that by not giving his father a chance to show him his attributes, he has hurt both his father and himself.

Episode#202: Change of a Dollar - March 13, 1983 - Director: Bob Lally - Writer/s: Michael G. Moye and Ron Leavitt - Guest/s: Mina Kolb, Bob Ari, John Del Regno, Peter Schrum (voice of George's first dollar), Berlinda Tolbert, Kate Ward.

Through the eyes of the first dollar Jefferson Cleaners brought in, we see George and Louise's joy and heartbreak opening their first store.

Episode#203: Designing Woman - March 20, 1983 - Director: Bob Lally - Teleplay by: Hans Kracauer - Story by: Ilene Cooper & Patrick Egan - Guest/s: Berlinda Tolbert, Georgann Johnson

Jenny is furious with George for trying to push her fashion sketches on a top designer. But when George tears one of the designer's gowns, Jenny stays up all night repairing it. Jenny does such beautiful work the designer offers her a job.

Episode#204: Double Trouble - March 27, 1983 - Director: Bob Lally - Writer/s: Ilene Cooper & Patrick Egan - Guest/s: Stephanie Braxton, Randy Earlie, Phil Boroff, Bonnie Mirliss, Lynne Marie Stewart, John Dewey Carter

To combat Cunningham's celebrity campaign, George hires look-a-likes to endorse Jefferson Cleaners. To teach George a lesson, Louise hires a look-a-like TV woman to expose George's scam.

Episode#205: Silver Lining - April 3, 1983 - Director: Bob Lally - Teleplay by: Peter Casey & David Lee - Story by: Jerry Perzigian & Donald L. Seigel - Guest/s: Peggy McCay (McCay played Caroline Brady on *Days of Our Lives* from 1983 to 2016)

When Florence finds $2,500 in the lining of a rummage sale hat, she learns that she must wait a certain amount of time before it is legally hers. The rightful owner appears and claims the money. Florence is disappointed until she learns that the coat that came with the hat contains $25,000 and she receives a ten percent reward for finding it.

Episode#206: The Wheel of Forever - April 20, 1983 - Director: Bob Lally - Writer/s: Sandy Sprung & Marcy Vosburgh - Guest/s: Berlinda Tolbert, Rob Stone (TV announcer voice)

After a bitter argument with Florence about buying her a new TV set, George falls asleep and dreams he died and is a contestant in a game show, playing for the way he will spend eternity. Florence appears as God and when George awakens, he promises to buy her the TV.

Episode#207: Personal Business - May 1, 1983 - Director: Bob Lally - Teleplay by: Marcy Vosburgh & Sandy Sprung - Story by: Lewis Goldstein - Guest/s: No guests

Louise, upset that she and George no longer spend time alone together, insists they go bicycling in the park where they each break a leg. Florence is away which means they are totally alone while their breaks heal.

END OF SEASON NINE EPISODES

Norman Lear was quoted as saying, "People are now watching without thinking Black or White," and that "The scripts have remained consistently interesting and funny." He thought that the comic timing was as good as anything he had ever seen. Lear gave much of the credit for the show being rated #9 to the relationship between the actors both onstage and offstage. The actors also had good communication with the producers.

Roxie Roker and Franklin Cover no longer share the screen on the opening credits; they are both listed on the screen by themselves. Berlinda Tolbert is listed as a guest during this season. Paul Benedict is not listed.

As the years passed Tom and George started getting along more, by Season Nine they had become friends. As Tom put it: "It's the Laurel and Hardy syndrome. I'm still gullible, but he doesn't call me as many names anymore."

However, there seemed to be faint stirrings that *The Jeffersons* might be winding down. There were certainly questions. In answer to a question from an interviewer, Franklin Cover had this to say: "Actors never feel secure unless you're Paul Newman or Robert Redford. I don't have a contract for next year—I assume I'd be back – but I don't kow {sic}." Cover felt that every year the show was going to end. "Critics hate us, but no matter what they say viewers watch us."

Maybe the stirrings came about because famous well-known guests began to make special appearances; guests like Gladys Knight (the Empress of Soul), Garrett Morris (*Saturday Night Live*) and Johnny Brown (Bookman from *Good Times*). In TV talk, according to the internet, this sort of tact is called "stunting". It is normally used to help a show survive. Also, because of a timeslot change *The Jeffersons* was now competing with *The A-Team*, and Mr. T was very compelling.

During this season the *Alton-Telegraph* asked Sanford about her hopes in the longevity of *The Jeffersons:* Isabel Sanford hopes *The Jeffersons* will make it to a decade - "I'd like to round out 10 years with the series. As long as the writers don't go dry, we can make it. And if they do go dry, we'll get fresh ones."

If a situation comedy is not funny the viewers stop tuning in and the ratings drop. In the nine years *The Jeffersons* had been on the air, I imagine there must have been one or two episodes that did not provide cheer for everyone. For me it was "Heeeere's Johnny." Possibly because the Johnny character is a chauvinistic, loudmouthed, annoying man, and he tells terrible jokes. Of course, that was the point of this week's show, which means that Johnny Brown played his part perfectly. Brown was a favorite at the time because of another Lear sitcom, *Good Times*.

I did not find this Johnny character funny. Chauvinism does not make me want to laugh. In 1982, the same year of the above episode, there was an article by a doctor who claimed that women were unfit to be in a position of leadership because of their raging hormonal imbalances. I wonder if the writers were aware of this social problem at the time and used it as inspiration. Chauvinism at the time did not seem to lend itself to hilarity. Of course, I am just one woman but others in the audience may have shared my feelings, which could have led to slightly less interest in the program.

The show did get funnier when Tom got a chance to imitate Lionel Barrymore in "True Confessions." George and Louise had been sponsoring a foster child, little Jimmie, and he was coming to visit his mom and dad. Turns out little Jimmie was a 40-year-old man (played by Garrett Morris) who had lied in an ad asking for help ten years earlier. The outcome of this meeting provides a lot of positivity and some gifts for a children's charity. Some people today think the idea of bringing Morris into the show was a sort of last-ditch effort to help the show's ratings, but Morris was a funny man. As a matter of fact, he is still performing almost 40 years later.

Whether it was to boost ratings or not, the guest on the 200th episode of *The Jeffersons* was one of the most loved and well-known R&B singers of the 60s, 70s, and 80s, Gladys Knight. She had recorded multiple major hits, one of which ("I Heard it Through the Grapevine") won her an Emmy. During her appearance as herself in "The Good Life," the recording of that song was played. Because everything is going so well at the Jeffersons, Florence decides to treat herself to a day at the spa. She meets Gladys Knight at the spa, but does not realize it, and after having a conversation with this woman, Florence tips the spa assistant extra for the lady because Knight has let Florence believe she is a struggling working woman. Later that evening, Knight shows up at the apartment to thank her. Knight still boosts ratings today.

Following Ms. Knight's visit was "Father's Day." The importance of this episode is more about how *The Jeffersons* helped an actor in his personal life. Guest Norman D. Wilson, a paraplegic actor, had appeared in *The Stone Killer* starring Charles Bronson in 1973. Wilson had spent the last thirteen years in a wheelchair. *The Jeffersons*' producers cast Wilson as Ray Taylor, a wheelchair-bound contractor who is George and Louise's new upstairs neighbor. This acting opportunity came at the perfect time for Wilson who had been helping his 12-year-old daughter fight a serious case of ovarian cancer while struggling with landlords who wanted to evict him from his two-bedroom apartment in Los Angeles because he could not pay the rent. In this instance, *The Jeffersons* was instrumental in helping a person in need. Though this may not have been known by the viewers, the fact that it happened certainly improved Wilson's situation at the time.

Episode #202: "Change of a Dollar" was a particular favorite of mine. If the flashback to how George earned his first dollar in the cleaning business was meant to renew interest using nostalgia, it worked. First, I have to say I loved the hairdos. George had gone to his cleaning establishment to count his money which he did every Thursday, to reassure himself that he was still wealthy. (By the way, Jeffersons Cleaners takes VISTA credit cards.) George's first dollar (voiced by actor Peter Schrum) is hanging on the wall. The dollar is the narrator of this flashback: "Hi, I'm the first dollar George ever made. Today he is the same little guy he was fifteen years ago." The flashback begins: It's the Grand Opening of Jefferson Cleaners and George has sprung for snacks and wine (in a six-pack) for his customers. In celebration, he informs Weezy that he is making her a 50% owner of the cleaners. He tells her he is looking forward to making money and sending Lionel to college. It's almost 7:00 and he is waiting for his first customer, and waiting, and waiting.

Finally, he gets his first customer, Mrs. Cody. She shares that she is using his establishment to support the "little guy" but that she won't be in the neighborhood much longer as her husband is doing well financially, and they are planning to move to a better part of town. Before leaving the store, she asks George for change for a dollar. George gives it to her. Sometime later Mrs. Cody, now grey-haired, and still using Jefferson Cleaners in Queens, comes to pick up her cleaning. Her husband has died, and her finances have dwindled. She has no money to pay. George agrees to put it on her account and then he tears up her bill. The dollar speaks: "Yep, same thing every Thursday, not a bad guy, huh?"

Peter Schrum, prior to voicing George's first dollar, had appeared in the TV program "Gimme a Break," and was the Coca-Cola Santa Claus for ten years.

I have a friend who once wrote for *The Jeffersons*. We recently talked about the fact that sitcoms usually only ran for seven seasons. The fact that *The Jeffersons* was now in its ninth season was a testament to its success as a sitcom. There was a uniqueness to this show. Something that grabbed the viewers and drew them in causing them to be curious about next week's program. People liked visiting *The Jeffersons*.

Chapter Fifteen:
Season Ten

Episode#208: Mission Incredible, Pt. 1 - October 2, 1983 - Director: Oz Scott - Writer/s: Michael G. Moye - Guest/s: Garrett Morris, Jason Bernard, Peter Iacangelo, Stefan Gierasch, Greg Morris

George has a reunion with some old navy buddies and the fact that Tom has become so gullible becomes a topic of discussion. This leads his old pals to talk George into playing a little con game on Tom. The con game becomes a bit too real when George's old pals make off with $15,000 of Tom's money.

Episode#209: Mission Incredible, Pt. 2 - October 3, 1983 - Director: Oz Scott - Writer/s: Michael G. Moye - Guest/s: Garrett Morris, Jason Bernard, Greg Morris, Stefan Gierasch

A furious Tom almost kills George when he learns he's been hustled out of money that he had planned to use to make a down payment on a house. George's friend Jimmy talks George and Tom into going to Los Angeles to meet his cousin who has a plan to get Tom's money back.

Episode#210: Mission Incredible, Pt. 3 - October 9, 1983 - Director: Oz Scott - Writer/s: Michael G. Moye - Guest/s: Garrett Morris, Jason Bernard, Greg Morris, Stefan Gierasch

Jimmy's cousin puts his plan into effect – a plan which includes getting the two thieves to believe that Los Angeles is going to be hit by a military attack from a neighboring country.

Episode#211: I Do, I Don't - October 16, 1983 - Director: Oz Scott - Writer/s: Jeffrey Richman and Joyce Gittlin - Guest/s: David Paymer, Robin Pearson Rose, Helen Martin, Jon Gries, Rai Tasco, Grant Wilson, Lycia Naff, Sharee Gregory

Tom and Helen are hosting a seminar for newlyweds, a job that George learns that he could be doing if Louise hadn't passed on it without telling him. However, when Tom falls ill, George gets his chance.

Episode#212: How Not to Marry a Millionaire - October 23, 1983 - Director: Oz Scott - Writer/s: Kim Weiskopf - Guest/s: Robin Braxton, Bennet Guillory

Florence and her friend, Betty, go down to the museum in hopes of landing millionaires. Florence meets a man whose true intentions prove to be extremely painful to Florence.

Episode#213: And the Winner Is.... - October 30, 1983 - Director: Oz Scott - Writer/s: Neil Lebowitz - Guest/s: Dorothy Butts, Bumper Robins

Louise is eyeing the Help Center's Volunteer of the Year award. However, she is afraid she may not win as Mrs. Van Morris has donated $2,500 to the Help Center in her bid to win the award.

Episode#214: The Return of Bentley - November 6, 1983 - Director: Oz Scott - Writer/s: Peter Casey and David Lee - Guest/s: Jack Fletcher, John Considine, Aarika Wells, Sylvia Farrel, Joey Jupiter-Levin

Harry Bentley is returning to New York, and everyone is excited except George. George believes the new occupant of Bentley's old apartment could make him a lot of money.

Episode#215: The List - November 20, 1983 - Director: Oz Scott - Writer/s: Marty Farrell - Guest/s: Roosevelt Grier, Anna Young, Jay Scorpio, Ernie Lee Banks, Al White, John Wesley

George gets a letter from an old friend who had made a bet with George years ago that he could accomplish everything on his life goal list before George. George pulls out his old list and realizes there is one thing he hasn't done: get even with a childhood bully.

Episode#216: Who's the Fairest? - December 4, 1983 - Director: Oz Scott - Writer/s: Al Aidekman - Guest/s: Jack Fletcher, Deborah Burrell, Julie Brown, Darwyn Carson, Lana Clarkson, Ruby Handler, Danny Wells

For his latest promotion, George decides to hold a beauty contest to find "Miss Jefferson Cleaners". Whittendale wants George to pick his punk rocker niece.

Episode#217: Father Christmas - December 11, 1983 - Director: Oz Scott - Writer/s: Kevin Kelton and Jerry Perzigian & Donald L. Seigel - Guest/s: Christian Brackett-Zika, Larry O. Williams, Jr., James Avery, Garth Wilton, Jonathan Ian

After refusing to go Christmas caroling with Louise, Helen, Florence and Bentley, George and Tom sit at home decorating the tree. They reminisce about past Christmases with their fathers.

Episode#218: What Makes Sammy Run - January 1, 1984 - Director: Tony Singletary - Writer/s: Sara V. Finney - Guest/s: Sammy Davis, Jr., William G. Schilling

Louise discovers that Sammy Davis, Jr. is renting the apartment across the hall in order to get some peace and quiet from his fans.

Episode#219: Getting Back to Basiks - January 8, 1984 - Director: Tony Singletary - Writer/s: Rosalind Stevenson, Marcy Vosburgh & Sandy Sprung - Guest/s: Randy Brooks

George needs a new gimmick for his dry-cleaning business, so he decides to hire Walter, an artist, to put together an animated commercial.

Episode#220: The Command Post - January 15, 1984 - Director: Tony Singletary - Writer/s: Peter Casey & David Lee - Guest/s: Howard Mann, Stephen Furst, Conroy Gedeon, Bernadette Birkett, Susann Akers

Florence is sad because George and Louise are going on a vacation to Atlantic City without her. Florence ends up in the hospital when she lets police officers in to use the apartment as a stakeout.

Episode#221: Real Men Don't Dry Clean - January 28, 1984 - Director: Oz Scott - Writer/s: Ed Burnham and Elaine Newman - Guest/s: Michael Halsey, Gary Hayes, Dorian Gibbs

Louise, Helen, and Florence are in awe of the instructor of their self-defense class and his rugged ways. George and Tom decide that they too are manly and go on a hunting trip but wind up bringing home stuffed animals.

Episode#222: Trading Places - February 12, 1984 - Director: Oz Scott - Writer/s: Marcy Vosburgh & Sandy Sprung - Guest/s: Susan Kellermann

Louise has had it with George who breaks his previous engagements with Tom and Bentley to go golfing on Saturday. She daydreams about what it would be like to be in George's shoes and not care about the feelings of those around him.

Episode#223: My Guy, George - March 4, 1984 - Director: Oz Scott - Writer/s: Jerry Perzigian & Donald L. Seigel - Guest/s: Sister Sledge, Timothy Scott, Michael Talbott

Florence manages to get George to become the manager of a struggling singing sister group. George books them into a country western bar and the audience is less than welcoming.

Episode#224: A New Girl in Town - March 11, 1984 - Director: Oz Scott - Writer/s: Marty Farrell - Guest/s: Renn Woods **(See Interview with Renn Woods - Chapter Eighteen)** Kyle T. Heffner, Ed Call

Florence is excited when she learns her 18-year-old cousin Rhonda is coming to New York for a visit. Louise and Florence trick George into allowing her to stay with them. An argument with Florence leads Rhonda to move out.

Episode#225: Otis - March 18, 1984 - Director: Oz Scott - Writer/s: Michael G. Moye - Guest/s: Charles Lampkin, John Dewey Carter, Susie Garrett

George is excited about having a magazine expose done on him and his business. However, the magazine does not want to use the shoeshine man that George has picked to sing his praises.

Episode#226: Hart to Heart - March 25, 1984 - Director: Oz Scott - Writer/s: Jerry Perzigian & Donald L. Seigel - Guest/s: Jack Fletcher, Anita Keith, Myrna White, Lonnie Hirsch

Ralph, the doorman, wants a raise and Louise and George give him the confidence to ask Mr. Whittendale. Ralph gets the unexpected news that Whittendale is thinking of installing an automatic elevator!

Episode#227: George's Old Girl Friend - April 1, 1984 - Director: Oz Scott - Writer/s: Kurt Taylor - Guest/s: Barbara McNair

Louise finds a perfume-soaked letter in the mail to George from an old girlfriend.

Episode#228: Honeymoon Hotel - April 15, 1984 - Director: Oz Scott - Writer/s: Jerry Perzigian & Donald L. Seigel - Guest/s: Charles Tyner, Fred McGrath, Alice Cadogan

Tom and Helen's 30th wedding anniversary is anything but happy when they get into a big argument over where they should go to spend the day together.

Episode#229: In the Chips - May 6, 1984 - Director: Arlando Smith - Writer/s: Peter Casey & David Lee - Guest/s: Garrett Morris, Irwin Keyes, Ernestine Mercer, Carl M. Craig, Elma V. Jackson

George's old pal Jimmy arrives at the Jefferson's apartment with a bag full of gambling chips and a wild story of how he got them.

END OF SEASON TEN EPISODES

Though it was thought by some that ABC's *The A-Team* may have played a part in this season's dropped ratings, according to Isabel Sanford the show was still a ratings winner. In a *Joplin Globe-Ozarks* article she gave this explanation: "Number one, we all like each other. Two, we get good writers. There's a turnover in writers, but they're well-trained and they keep the flavor of the show. They know what Louise would say and not say. We have hit the heart of America. People tell me everywhere I go they love *The Jeffersons*."

We see that a real effort was made to inject some interest and excitement into the show by featuring these well-known personalities: Barbara McNair, a singer, television, and film actor. Roosevelt Grier, a championship football player. Grier was also host of the *The Rosey Grier Show*, a television and movie actor, and, in 1983, he became an ordained minister. Grier was also the man who removed the gun from the hand of the man who tried to assassinate Robert F. Kennedy. Sammy Davis, Jr., a man who needed no introduction, was also brought in as a guest.

This season Paul Benedict is back in the opening credits. Season Ten also brought us such stars as James Avery, who would later portray the father in the TV sitcom *Fresh Prince of Bel-Air*, Sister Sledge, a Grammy nominated R&B vocal group, Ren Woods who had previously appeared on TV in *Roots* and on the big screen in *Car Wash, Hair, The Jerk, Xanadu, 9 to 5*, and *Penitentiary II*, and was cast as Dorothy in a 1976 musical tour of *The Wiz*.

On December 4, 1983. Gibbs and Hemsley both received supporting TV awards in the 15th annual NAACP Image Awards. Would cast members receive awards if the show were losing steam? There were still good writers, though two of the staff writers that had been there since 1975, Jay Moriarty and Mike Milligan, had gone on to other ventures.

Garrett Morris and Greg Morris appeared in "Mission Incredible." This three-part episode provided laughs and fun memories. The writer of this episode, Michael G. Moye, was a writing genius, in my opinion, and proved it as he went on to help bring success to the television sitcom industry through his writing skills.

Garrett Morris had been in the business for many years, and before appearing on *The Jeffersons* was a regular on *Saturday Night Live* (SNL). Garrett Morris is a funny man. He had been in show business since 1960, in movies and numerous television shows. Morris is still working at his craft as of the writing of this book. Greg Morris was known for his role in *Mission Impossible.* Though it had been ten years since the series was on the air, Morris was still a fan favorite having gone on to appear in other television programs, including the TV detective series *VEGA$*.

As a viewer in the 1970s, I never concerned myself with whether these episodes were written by women or men. I realize now that most of the writers were men. Sara V. Finney is credited with having written "What Makes Sammy Run" and I think she did *The Jeffersons* proud. Of course, Sammy Davis, Jr., as himself, was perfect as the celebrity trying to relax away from his many fans. Too bad he runs into Louise in the hallway of their building. Louise promises to keep his presence in the building secret, but she cannot keep herself from bothering Sammy. Consequently, the poor man winds up on the balcony in the rain, stuffed in the closet and locked in the front bathroom. This episode is a bit silly and a lot of fun, just like Sammy Davis, Jr.

It should be noted that Louise had earlier briefly met Sammy (as himself) on an episode of *All in the Family*, when the Jeffersons were still neighbors of the Bunkers.

Along with the more well-known visible stars the show had to have some relevance to current issues and that meant they had to include storylines that referenced touchy subjects. After all, this was a show about a modern family and the day-to-day happenings in their lives. One issue back then, especially for Black people, was the issue of stereotyping.

Black people in the 1980s in America did not want to be seen as a "stereotype." Typically, the worry was that White people would portray Black people in stereotypical roles. In "Otis" there is a slightly different take on the idea. Black people saying bootblacks are stereotypical. There were very few Black writers on TV sitcoms back in 1984; this episode was written by a Black writer. Fun fact: Otis has a pendant hanging around his neck with a piece of coral in it – I believe the coral relates to someone involved with the writing of this episode.

"Otis" was the shoeshine man. George wants Otis to speak with a Black magazine that deals with successful Black people, to tell them about what he, Otis, thinks of George. When the magazine finds out Otis is a shoeshine man and not someone of a higher caliber, they refuse to interview him. George must give Otis the bad news. Otis points out to George that this is a case of Black people being racist against other Black people because they think shining shoes is something to be ashamed of; that this is an idea that someone has thought up, and that Blacks play into. As far as Otis was concerned, he saw himself as a working person who put his kids through college, just like any other working person. George begins to understand the concept as Otis sees it. At the end of this episode George is shining Otis's shoes.

The man who played Otis was Mr. Charles Lampkin. He was an actor, musician, and lecturer. From 1951 to 1988 he acted in many TV shows, such as *Surfside 6, Mr. Novak, Dr. Kildare, The Untouchables, The Wild, Wild West, It Takes a Thief, Julia, Highway to Heaven, 227* and many more. He also appeared in a few movies, such as *Watermelon Man, The Odd Couple, Cornbread, Earl and Me, Cocoon* and the list goes on. As a musician he composed a piano concerto in G minor and was a Professor of Music and Theater Arts at Santa Clara University. As an entertainer, Lampkin had a great deal of experience and added to the realism of Black life portrayed on *The Jeffersons*.

Chapter Sixteen:
Season Eleven

Episode#230: Blood and Money - October 4, 1984 - Director: Oz Scott - Writer/s: James Kutras, Jeffrey Richman, and Joyce Gittlin - Guest/s: Jack Fletcher, Gene Ross, Gino Conforti, Dorothy Butts

The Help Center is having a blood drive and Louise tries to get George to donate some. However, a leery George pays Ralph to give blood in his name. The blood saves the life of Mrs. Whittendale.

Episode#231: Ebony and Ivory - October 21, 1984 - Director: Oz Scott - Writer/s: Cheri Steinkellner & Bill Steinkellner - Guest/s: Ebonie Smith, Dorothy Butts, Jaleel White, Gino Conforti - Ebonie Smith's character was as the granddaughter Jessica Jefferson. She would appear in three additional episodes.

The snobby socialite that beat Louise out of a Volunteer of the Year award is back and brags about her grandson's piano recital. Louise decides to enter her granddaughter, Jessica.

Episode#232: Bobbles, Bungles, and Boo Boos - October 28, 1984 - Director: Oz Scott - Writer/s: Winston Moss - Guest/s: Terrence McGovern, Johnny Haymer, Gloria Charles, Judy Kerr, Marcia Del Mar, Suzanne LaRusch, Linda Darlow, Michael Prokopuk

Louise and Florence have the perfect plan to get the best of George. They've got a "hidden video" show coming over on the pretense of an interview with George, and the apartment gets robbed.

Episode#233: A House Divided - November 4, 1984 - Director: Oz Scott - Writer/s: Ann Gibbs and Joel Kimmel - Guest/s: Jack Fletcher, David Fresco, Dale Reynolds

Louise is running for tenant council president and is sure she is going to win.

Episode#234: Some Enchanted Evening - November 18, 1984 - Director: Arlando Smith - Writer/s Billy Dee Williams and Marla Gibbs (yes, Ms. Gibbs contributed as a writer), Marcy Vosburgh & Sandy Sprung - Guest/s: Hal Williams, Kip King, Becky Bonar, Gertrude Clement

George, Louise, Tom, and Helen go out to a big charity ball where Florence's favorite soap star is scheduled to appear. Unfortunately, Florence cannot go as all the tickets are sold out.

Episode#235: The Gift - November 25, 1984 - Director: Oz Scott - Writer/s: Bobby Herbeck - Guest/s: Danny Wells, Kip King

Louise is all excited that, for once, George has remembered her birthday after she sees him sneaking around with party favors.

Episode#236: They Don't Make Preachers Like Him Anymore - December 16, 1984 - Director: Oz Scott - Writer/s: Ron Leavitt and Michael G. Moye - Guest/s: Julius Harris, Rene Le Vant

Florence loses her faith in God when the Reverend of her church steals money meant for a trip to a choir singing competition.

Episode#237: Try A Little Tenderness - December 23, 1984 - Director: Oz Scott - Writer/s: Oz Scott and Joe Rosario - Guest/s: Pamela Adlon (credited as Segall), Tony La Torre, Michael Wyle, Millie Baron

After catching two young kids trying to break into their store, Louise bets George she can turn them around and he won't have to give her $2,000 to save the Help Center.

Time Slot Change: January 1985 - March 1985, from Sunday 9:30-10:00pm to Tuesday 8:00-8:30pm

Episode#238: You'll Never Get Rich - January 8, 1985 - Director: Oz Scott - Writer/s: Lewis Goldstein and Richard Kraut - Guest/s: Phyllis Diller, Charo, Engelbert Humperdinck, Helen Reddy, Joe Frazier and Michael Spinks, Michael Yama, Michael G. Hawkins, James F. Dean, Gloria Hayes, Deanna Oliver, Millie Baron, Rif Hutton

Florence accompanies George and Louise to Atlantic City where she is struck by gambling fever. Louise is determined to see some celebrities.

Episode#239: The Unnatural - January 15, 1985 - Director: Oz Scott - Writer/s: Andy Horowitz and Jerry Perzigian & Donald L. Seigel - Guest/s: Reggie Jackson, Brian Downing, Mike Witt, Peter Iacangelo, Bobby Herbeck, Joseph Savant

George drops Reggie Jackson's home run hit and suffers humiliation from insults. Louise has a plan to bolster his self-esteem.

Episode#240: The Chairman of the Bored - January 22, 1985 - Director: Oz Scott - Writer/s: Stu Goldman & Vito J. Giambalvo - Guest/s: Pam Newman, Trish Garland, Playboy Playmates-Marcy Hanson, Susie Scott, Michele Drake, Victoria Cooke, Denise Kellogg

When George, Louise and Helen are all busy, an ignored Tom gets all the attention he could want from the sister of Mr. Bentley's girlfriend.

Episode#241: Sayonara, Pt. 1 - January 29, 1985 - Director: Oz Scott - Writer/s: Peter Casey & David Lee - Guest/s: Mike Evans, Berlinda Tolbert, Ebonie Smith

Lionel and Jenny return to New York after a trip to Japan and they have an announcement. They've decided to get a divorce.

Episode#242: Sayonara, Pt. 2 - February 6, 1985 - Director: Oz Scott - Writer/s: Cheri Eichen & Bill Steinkellner - Guest/s: Mike Evans, Berlinda Tolbert, Peter Jacobs, Peggy Blow, Lindy Nisbet

After hearing the news of the divorce, George and Louise get into a fight with Tom and Helen and the fight continues all the way through Family Night at Jessica's school.

Episode#243: Last Dance - February 12, 1985 - Director: Oz Scott - Writer/s: Cheri Eichen & Bill Steinkellner - Guest/s: Larry B. Scott, Penny Johnson Jerald, Stoney Jackson, Jere Fields, Crystal Jenious

George's assistant, Clark, does not have a date for the prom and Florence agrees to attend the prom with him.

Episode#244: The Gang's All Here - February 19, 1985 - Director: Oz Scott - Writer/s: Al Aidekman - Guest/s: Danny Wells, Warren Berlinger, Reid Shelton, William Bronder, Bill Marcus, Dick Yammy, Steve Susskind

Charlie the bartender goes out of town for the weekend and Louise agrees to take his place for a special party. Turns out it is a reunion of a biker gang.

Episode#245: Hail to the Chief - March 12, 1985 - Director: Oz Scott - Writer/s: Hans Kracauer - Guest/s: Patience Cleveland, R. J. Miller, Herb Vigran, Tim Silva

Tom is up for promotion to President of Pelham Publishing and is afraid he will not get it. But after getting the promotion he begins to consider resigning because of the pressure.

Episode#246: A Secret in the Back Room - March 19, 1985 - Director: Oz Scott - Writer/s: Jerry Perzigian & Don Seigel - Guest/s: Danny Wells, Mike Evans, Berlinda Tolbert

George and Louise's anniversary party is interrupted when they learn that Charlie, the bartender, has a drinking problem.

Time Slot Change: April 1985, from Tuesday 8:00-8:30pm to Tuesday 8:30-9:00pm

Episode#247: That Blasted Cunningham - April 2, 1985 - Director: Oz Scott - Writer/s: Mark Zakarin and Peter Casey & David Lee - Guest/s: Susan Ruttan, Pierrinno Mascarino, Dave Shelley, Richard Foronjy, Tak Kubota, Billy Beck

In an advertising war, George and Cunningham Cleaners have vowed to out promote the other.

Episode#248: State of Mind - April 23, 1985 - Director: Oz Scott - Writer/s: Cheri Eichen & Bill Steinkellner - Guest/s: Kathleen Wilhoite, Mary Jackson, Elmarie Wendel, Fred Carney

Louise is accused of being an "old fuddy-duddy" when she complains about her young neighbor's constant partying.

Episode#249: And Up We Go - April 30, 1985 - Director: Oz Scott - Writer/s: Warren S. Murray and Cheri Eichen & Bill Steinkellner - Guest/s: Luise Heath, Edie McClurg

George and Tom decide to break a record by seeing how many times they can go up and down in an elevator.

Final Time Slot Change: June 1985- July 1985, from Tuesday 8:30-9:00pm to Tuesday 8:00-8:30pm

Episode#250: The Truth Hurts - June 4, 1985 - Director: Paul Benedict - Writer/s: Stephen Neigher and Sarah V. Finney & Vida Spears - Guest/s: Danny Wells, Oliver Clark, Cal Gibson

Louise finishes her painting in Art Class, and everyone lies to her about what they really think of the painting. Louise is so happy she considers putting on an art show.

Episode#251: The Odd Couple - June 11, 1985 - Director: Michael G. Moye - Writer/s: Peter Casey & David Lee - Guest/s: Susie Garrett, Ellen Gerken

Florence places an ad in a personals column and winds up meeting Bentley.

Episode#252: Off-Off-Off-Off Broadway - June 25, 1985 - Director: Oz Scott - Writer/s: Matt Robinson - Guest/s: George McGrath, Julius Carry III, Steve Devorkin **(See interview with Steve Devorkin - Chapter Eighteen)**, Jennifer Barlow, Jackie Roth (credited as Hinner)

To raise cash to save the Disabled Youth Services program, Louise and Helen decide to put on a talent show. This episode was written to showcase each cast member in a variety show format: Sanford, Roker & Gibbs singing, Benedict doing impressions, Cover putting on a slide show, and Hemsley playing the flute.

Episode#253: Red Robins - July 2, 1985 - Director: Oz Scott - Writer/s: Peter Casey & David Lee and Cheri Eichen & Bill Steinkellner - Guest/s: Ebonie Smith, Phil Rubenstein, Dinah Lacey, Virginya Keehne, Keri Houlihan, Penina Segall and Bridget Sienna

George wants the Dry Cleaner of the Year award but needs to have some experience in community service. He decides to take over as "nest mother" for his granddaughter's Red Robin troop.

END OF SEASON ELEVEN EPISODES

In this, the last season, the following may have been two reasons that the show was cancelled: CBS moved the show from Sundays to Tuesdays, 8:00-9:00 p.m. This was known as the "killer 8-to-9" time slot. *The Jeffersons* were now competing with *The A-Team, Cheers, The Cosby Show, Facts of Life, Highway to Heaven, Knight*

Rider, Hunter, Hill St. Blues and *Miami Vice*; Morgan Gendel of *The Los Angeles Times* wrote that "the show's license fee (the amount the production company charges the network for each episode) increased each year, and that as a result, *The Jeffersons* in its 11th season was one of TV's more expensive half hours."

Harvey Shephard, Senior Vice President for Programming, had called the show "tired." Gibbs objected to that label. "I don't know what was wrong with Harvey Shephard's mouth when he said *The Jeffersons* was tired. We're not tired. I'd just seen him the week before he said that, and he sure knew I wasn't tired."

According to Roker the show continued to undergo microscopic critiques from Blacks. People were saying that the show was "hampered by slapstick acting, stereotype roles and simplistic, even insulting, motivations." She, and the rest of the cast, felt that the show was still a success, the Jeffersons being an upwardly mobile family, and that family being intact. Father was head of the family and owning and operating a business. Roker's explanation for *The Jeffersons* durability, "We're not playing on one note anymore."

This season was different in that the insults were not as sharp. Per Gibbs: "We still do it, but I figure it's a mistake for me to attack him. Florence should be on the defensive. The best way is to make it like good-natured teasing. The writers make the mistake sometimes of depending too much on the one-liners." Gibbs noted that the show was still "evolving."

Faith, divorce, possible childhood danger, and alcoholism, are universal problems. Presenting them on television is a way to share empathy, hope and solutions. Add to that something that will elicit at least one laugh, and the viewers remain loyal. Add more celebrities and the viewers would be delighted, though Morgan Gendel, of *The Los Angeles Times* may not have agreed.

In a February 1985 article Gendel noted that "*The Jeffersons* had resorted to stunting (having the cast members going to Atlantic City and the casinos, meeting celebrities such as Charo, Helen Reddy, Michael Spinks, and bringing in several real Playboy playmates)."

By January of 1985, writers for *The Jeffersons* were running out of good ideas. I had stopped watching television during that time, so

I did a bit of looking back via the internet. I wondered if the writers could have gotten material from the major events of 1985, one of which was the recording by the super group USA for Africa of "We Are the World." The song was an instant hit, becoming the fastest selling U. S. pop single in history. To my way of thinking this happening would have lent itself very well to one or two good episodes, and maybe it did. "We Are the World" was sung by some of the most well-known musical artists of that time. Perhaps it played some small part in this season's "You'll Never Get Rich" episode by using well-known celebrities to dazzle and entertain.

Stunting it may have been, but they certainly picked great entertainers. There was Phyllis Diller, a much loved stand-up comedian (I still remember her joke about her daughter answering the front door and telling the PTA woman that her mother was in the kitchen hitting the bottle, she didn't mention it was the ketchup bottle); Charo, the beautiful uninhibited flamenco "cuchi-cuchi" dancer; Engelbert Humperdink who, at the time, performed over 200 concerts a year; Helen Reddy, who had won a Grammy Award for her 1972 hit "I Am Woman"; "Smokin" Joe Frazier, the first boxer to beat Muhammad Ali in "The Fight of the Century" in 1971; and Michael Spinks who became the first light-heavyweight champion to win the world heavyweight title. They were all on hand in Atlantic City when Florence got bitten by the gambling bug. One thing about this story is Gibbs as Florence had the best role. Florence had proven to be the one character that kept the audience's interest.

The Jeffersons ability to mix the serious with the silly was on display in "They Don't Make Preachers Like Him Anymore." Florence's faith in the church and in those who minister the congregation is tested. Reverend Taylor (Julius Harris) is out ill, and Reverend Harris is brought in temporarily. Reverend Harris absconds with the church's donations that were to be used for a trip to a choir competition. Florence is a member of the choir, and her show of disappointment causes George to want to console her by quoting the Bible, which is where the humor comes in. George is not good with Biblical references, but his ignorance provides a good laugh. George asks Florence if she remembers Sodom and Gomorrah, "They had it all together until Gomorrah cut off Sodom's hair. So, not only did Sodom lose his faith but that also brought about the wisdom of Sodom, so he had to spend the rest of his days sleeping on a pillow of salt." I do not know if this was written into the script or ad-libbed but it sure was funny.

The miraculous ending produced goose bumps when I saw it. Florence decides to remove her belongings from the church and while she was there the Reverend Taylor stops by and talks with her about the difference between faith in people and faith in her church. At the end we learn that Reverend Taylor had died four hours earlier.

The actor who played Reverend Taylor, Julius Harris, got his start in 1964 in the movie "Nothing But a Man" with Ivan Dixon and Abbey Lincoln, after which his career blossomed. He appeared in at least seven movies, including *Super Fly* (1972), *Black Caesar* (1973) and *Live and Let Die* (1973), and numerous television series, including *Cagney & Lacey*, *Hart to Hart*, *Benson* and *St. Elsewhere*.

Maybe nothing could have changed the timing of *The Jeffersons* cancellation, but the idea of bringing in the Playboy Playmates was, to me, incongruous. "The Chairman of the Bored" featured Tom Willis alone and bored in the apartment. He has no one to listen to his stories and he begins to daydream about being the center of attention. In this dream he gets a visit from five Playboy Bunnies who simply cannot get enough of Tom's stories. They fix his drinks, fan him and hover around him, hanging onto his every word. He loves it. Tom's daydream ends as Helen returns home. She feels badly about ignoring him and she apologizes. They hug. The end.

As if to make up for the less than interesting playmate episode, episodes over the next two weeks proved to be extremely moving. Ebonie Smith as Jessica Jefferson won viewers' hearts with her portrayal of the daughter of Lionel and Jenny. Lionel is returning home after spending three years on a job in Japan. Jenny had spent the last month with him. In "Sayonara" the two visit their parents with some surprising news. They are getting a divorce. The news causes a major rift between their parents which leads to an argument at Family Night at Jessica's school. Jessica had planned to show them a picture she had drawn of the family, but they are so intent on insulting each other she tears up the picture and leaves the room.

Panic sets in when it is realized that Jessica is not at the school. What they do not know is that she has walked the three blocks back to the Jefferson's apartment and is with Florence. In Pt. 2, Lionel gets angry and lets Tom, Helen, George, and Louise know how he feels about the way they have acted and how they have hurt Jessica. Louise explains that it is so difficult to accept the divorce and she begins to cry. The show ends after Louise apologizes to Jessica for upsetting her and everyone makes up, and together they glue Jessica's family picture back together.

This episode brought back memories of the day my own daughter left school and walked home by herself because she had forgotten her homework and did not want to get in trouble. As a matter of fact, she walked home and then walked back to school. She was about six or seven years old. I was at work when I received a call from the school letting me know what happened. My first thought was that anything could have happened to her. I left my job and went straight to the school. As a parent, knowing your child has been out in the streets by themselves is very traumatic. Another example of Lear's desire to produce a show "dealing with the problems American families were facing."

By now it must have been evident that *The Jeffersons* would not last much longer. The ratings had dropped from #19 to # 59. What they needed was more drama, that is what viewers were tuning into this year. But car chases and people getting beaten up did not fit well within a show like *The Jeffersons*. However, a story about a bartender would fit in as through the years the tenants of the Whittendale Building had spent many an evening in the building's bar. "The Secret in the Backroom" gave Charlie the bartender a chance to get out from behind the bar and just be a regular guy with a personal problem who could probably use some help. It is revealed that Charlie, played by Danny Wells, while running a successful bar, has struggled for years with a drinking problem, and is separated from his wife because of it; George and Louise help him to come to grips with the problem while preparing for their marriage anniversary party.

Charlie has been invited to the party and he decides to drop off a special bottle of wine before the party starts. He and Florence decide that Charlie should keep it downstairs in the bar until the party starts. He says he will keep it next to his bed. He admits to Florence that he is sleeping in the backroom of the bar because his wife has put him out because he is an alcoholic. Later, when Florence goes looking for Charlie, she finds that he has emptied the bottle of wine. Charlie shares his problem with Florence, who tells George and Louise. The upshot is that Charlie is convinced to go to the local help center. The subject was relevant to society's woes and had a positive ending, but it did not stop the cancellation.

In April of 1985, Morgan Gendel of *The Los Angeles Times*, wrote that Franklin Cover told him, "We have four more shows to do and we're still plugging away. If we are going out, we're going out with all guns firing." Someone knew something was up.

Gibbs had been in talks about starring in her own sitcom titled *227*. It had been decided that production would start in 1986. At the time of the talks *The Jeffersons* was still on the air. Gibbs was surprised when the cancellation was announced; however, it meant that she was able to start work on *227* a year earlier than expected.

Roker, in a 1984 interview, had admitted that she did not feel secure despite the show's long run; said she knew that as an actor, you could always be replaced; Devorkin, the actor who played the gnome in the next to last episode told me in our interview that he had detected discomfort among the cast members regarding whether *The Jeffersons* would be picked up the next season. As Devorkin was basically focusing on how his career was going to explode after this exposure, the sense of discomfort must have been great to penetrate his personal musings.

On May 8, 1985, the news of the cancellation came out in a *Los Angeles Times* article written by Lee Margulies. Per the article, "the series was cancelled by announcement at the CBS network "upfront" presentation the day before, nearly two months before the airing of the final episode." It was said that the cancellation came as no surprise because ratings for the show had fallen badly. "It ranked 59th among the 96 prime-time series that aired on the networks. It was believed that syndication (of the first four years) was one of the factors keeping viewers from watching the new episodes therefore lowering the ratings."

Though the cancellation had been mentioned in the newspaper in May, the cast and crew members were surprised as they were not officially informed until two months after the July 2, 1985 episode aired. Not only was the cancellation a surprise, but there was also no "final farewell episode." Sanford was never happy about not having a final farewell episode, especially after an eleven-season run. No way for the cast and crew to say goodbye to their fans. No satisfactory ending for fans who had been tuning in since January 1975. *The Jeffersons* simply went off the air. "Red Robins" episode #253 was the last episode to be aired in front of a live studio audience.

Chapter Seventeen:
After the Show

Of course, time takes its toll on all of us. We get older, lose our hair, wigs start looking like wigs. We run out of ideas. But, in the years after the cancellation, members of the cast would continue to receive recognition from fans, and from the media. They would appear in new sitcoms, show up at special events, and perform on stage. As happens in life, we have lost cast members from both *All in the Family* and *The Jeffersons*: Writers, producers, directors, and crew members. Here I have listed a bit of information about the principal players after the cancellation of *The Jeffersons*.

1985

Sanford appeared in the 19th annual MDA Labor Day telethon.

Sanford narrated 'The Patchwork Quilt,' on Reading Rainbow.

Hemsley was the emcee for the grand opening of Classy Cleaners, Inc. in the Courtyard Shopping Center. Customers were invited to bring their dry cleaning and a chair, enjoy food, drinks, and music from noon until 10 p.m. and be entertained by 'George' from 3 to 7 p.m., in New Braunfels, Texas.

1986

In one *Jeffersons* episode, George performs CPR on a Ku Klux Klan member. When her 14-month-old daughter Crystal was pulled unconscious from a backyard wading pool on July 9, 1986, in San Antonio, Texas, Dorothy Acosta remembered the CPR movements George performed in the episode, and in the process, saved her little girl's life. "Without that show," said Acosta, "she wouldn't be here." After Hemsley learned of the rescue (a reporter for the *San Antonio Light* contacted Hemsley's publicist), he made a phone call to Acosta and sent her an autographed picture.

Roxie Roker, the best thing in *Legends* at the Ahmanson in 1986, replaced Marla Gibbs in *Checkmates*, at the Westwood Playhouse.

1987
Sanford taping five shows a week of *Honeymoon Hotel*.

1988
Sanford and Roker at "A Salute to Biddy Mason and Black Leaders" (Mason was one of the founders of Los Angeles' first black church - the First A.M.E.). At event, major political, business and entertainment figures modeled furs, jewels, and clothes from their own wardrobes. Sanford and Roker modeled together.

At the 20th annual NAACP Image Awards, Hemsley received an award for Best Actor in a Comedy Series for his work on *Amen*.

Hemsley and Jane Curtin appeared in a special celebrating the 50th anniversary of *Snow White and the Seven Dwarfs*.

Roker guest-starred on Gibbs' *227*. Played Gibbs' high school friend, now a famous psychologist.

1989
Roker was on stage at the Inner-City Cultural Center's play, *Woman from the Town*, a play by Samm-Art Williams concerning a Black family in rural North Carolina.

Hemsley in Miami New Year's Eve parade. He wore flashing sunglasses and was backed by three female singers on a float celebrating Ben Franklin and electricity.

Hemsley had a repeating voiceover role on the puppet series *Dinosaurs* in the early '90s. He and Sanford reunited in commercials for *Old Navy*, *Gap*, and *Denny's*.

1991
Hemsley appeared on *All New Circus of the Stars & Side Show*" on CBS.

1993
The stage show titled *The Best of the Jeffersons* opened in Detroit. Hemsley, Sanford, Gibbs, Roker, and Cover appeared together again. There was no final episode of *The Jeffersons* to resolve all the loose ends, so that was another reason for the stage show. Getting

a little more respect and recognition was another motive. Laughed Marla Gibbs, "another reason was to make some money."

Hemsley and Sanford took 'The Jeffs' on a six-city roadshow tour with *The Jeffersons Live: The Movin' On Up Tour*. The show featured five original Jeffersons cast members doing three classic episodes from the series. Sanford: "We're on the air in Italy. We met our voice dubbers. Two little people, so happy to see us." *Times-News*, Burlington, N.C.

1995

Hemsley and Sanford reprised their roles as George and Louise on *The Fresh Prince of Bel-Air*. The Bel-Air mansion was for sale and George and Louise were prospective buyers.

Roxie Roker dies on December 2.

Hemsley and Sanford played husband and wife on the December 11th Christmas episode of *In the House*. Sanford was Debbie Allen's one-time-mother-in-law on the show.

2001

Carroll O'Connor dies June 21.

2003

Per Sherman Hemsley: Isabel Sanford gave Hemsley a funny look when first meeting him; she told him later that she expected a much larger man. She was their "Queen Bee". He said that all the cast had great relationships. He, Franklin, and Paul joked a lot - sometimes it was hard to do the serious parts. Lear came around on Wednesday. It was a blessing when he came. His character came out with the writing. *Burbank Bibliography Citation*: Sherman Hemsley Interview, by Karen Herman on August 17, 2003, for *TelevisionAcademy.com/Interviews*. *The Interviews: An Oral History of Television*.

2004

Isabel Sanford received a star on the Hollywood Walk of Fame in January.

Isabel Sanford dies July 9.

2006
Franklin Cover dies February 5.

2007
Gordon Mitchell's book, *Hackensack to Hollywood* was published by BearManor Media.

2008
Paul Benedict dies December 1.

2012
Sherman Hemsley was found dead on July 24.

2013
Jean Stapleton dies March 31.
Danny Wells (real name Jack Westelman) dies November 28.

2015
Andrew Rubin dies October 5.

2019
Jay Moriarty publishes his book *Honky in the House*. *His book is seen as* a fascinating look into the inner workings of *The Jeffersons*.

2020
Marla Gibbs made a surprise appearance in the May 2020 "Live in Front of a Studio Audience: Norman Lear's *All in the Family* and *The Jeffersons* reboot.

Norman Lear celebrated his 98th Birthday.

2021
Marla Gibbs celebrated her 90th Birthday.

Marla Gibbs is honored with a star by The Hollywood Chamber of Commerce on the Hollywood Walk of Fame on July 20, 2021, at 6840 Hollywood Blvd.

July 20, 2021, is declared Marla Gibbs Day in Hollywood

Chapter Eighteen:
Interviews

Norman Lear – Producer and Creator

I spoke with Norman Lear in January of 2019 (he was in his office, and I was at a park) via telephone. From our interview: Regarding the cast of *The Jeffersons*, Mr. Lear found Marla Gibbs to be "the greatest actress during the time of his career." He said she had "far more feeling as being human in this character than he can put into words." He thought Zara Cully, who portrayed "Mother" Jefferson, "funny as any human being - without saying a word." He said he found Sherman Hemsley a very "sweet" person. Not at all like the character he had portrayed. He thought Roxie Roker, who played Helen Willis, the Black character that was married to a White man, played by Franklin Cover, a "lovely woman". Mr. Lear related this conversation he had with Ms. Roker while interviewing her for the part: He told her that she would be required to "kiss and hug" her White husband as part of the show. He didn't know that Ms. Roker was married to a White man in real life. She said to him, "Let me answer you this way", whereupon she showed him a picture of her and her White husband.

Fun Fact: Quotation from George Orwell on the wall of Lear's office: "If liberty means anything at all, it means the right to tell people what they do not want to hear."

Berlinda Tolbert - Actor

I had the immense pleasure of interviewing Ms. Tolbert on October 1, 2019. I found her to be an easy person to talk with, which means I was not nervous in her presence. She had ordered lunch on her terrace, and we proceeded to have a lovely couple of hours discussing *The Jeffersons*.

We discussed how she got her agent. She was sitting in a waiting room, and someone asked her if she was an actress; when she answered "yes" she was asked if she had an agent. She said "no" and then he asked her if she wanted one. She answered "yes". The person was Booking Agent John Fisher.

She got work in some commercials. Then it was "off to San Francisco to do *Strays*". Mike Evans was playing opposite her and that is how she got the opportunity to play Jenny. Ms. Tolbert auditioned for the part of Jenny on only a minute's notice. Tolbert was shopping when, after checking her answering service, she found she had an urgent message to call her agent. The agent had lined her up for an audition. She had ten minutes to get there. Fortunately, she was in the area, but her appearance was not the best. She had no make-up, her hair was hidden by a floppy hat, and she was wearing a pair of old blue jeans. She described her appearance as "tacky." This echoes an interview done in 1975: "Berlinda Tolbert Gets First Television Part," Saturday, February 1, 1975, *Florence Morning News*, Florence, South Carolina, (this article edited by Ms. Tolbert in interview with this author: Joked Tolbert when she got the part, "At least I know I wasn't selected for this role because of my looks or a fancy wardrobe."

Ms. Tolbert was always aware of the effort put into the success of this show by the writers. In an April 1975 interview with Doris Worsham, *Tribune* Staff Writer, she said: "It takes a lot of writing to introduce people yet entertain the public at the same time." During our interview she mentioned one of the original writers of *The Jeffersons*, Gordon "Whitey" Mitchell, remembering him as "a wonderful guy," and she said she was deeply sorry to hear when he passed in 2009. We spoke of another of the original writers, Don Nicholl, and how he and his wife Gee had created a scholarship fund for screenwriters. About Sherman Hemsley, Ms. Tolbert said he was "the exact opposite of the character George Jefferson." "He was shy, gentle and respectful." Ms. Tolbert, Paul Benedict, and Roxie Roker would visit each other at their respective homes from time to time as they all lived in the general vicinity. She and Marla Gibbs became and remain, friends.

Regarding her friendship with her co-star Mike Evans, on and off the set, Tolbert stated they were "good friends, everyone liked him, he had charm and he was extremely likeable." Between takes on the set the two of them would fill the time by finding fun things to do, such as taking sailing lessons. When her character, Jenny, got pregnant, Tolbert made Mike go to (real) Lamaze classes with her at a hospital in Los Angeles.

We discussed some of the people who worked on the show offstage. Because of schedules limited by time given and deadlines, shows like *The Jeffersons* would not be as successful without these essential behind-the-scenes crew members. People like costumers Rita Riggs, Betsey Potter, Adela Farmer, and hair stylist Ray Hall, the gentleman Tolbert found while strolling down Sunset Boulevard one day. She had decided to get her hair conditioned before going to the set (though the producers had never and would never say anything to her about her hair or her clothes). She stepped into a salon and found Ray Hall. Mr. Hall turned out to be a brilliant, talented, creative hairdresser. She fell in love with this gentleman and felt he "would fit into *The Jeffersons* umbrella." On the set she went on and on about him until he was given a chance to show his talents. Mr. Hall eventually also got a chance to perform for a Vidal Sassoon show, the first time an African American had that opportunity. Mr. Hall would remain the hair stylist from 1979 until the last episode in 1985.

Tolbert has acted on stage and on television programs other than *The Jeffersons*; however she does not see herself as a star. She is an actor. In her words she is "not a dilettante." This is due in part to what she learned while on *The Jeffersons*. In answer to my question about what she learned while on the show, Tolbert stated "TV efficiency - the mechanics of TV." She learned "to be flexible and positive." She learned "to be amiable and gracious."

She "learned camaraderie." She "learned how to welcome guests to help their creativity." She was able to take these things to other sets within their filming studio. Tolbert looks back fondly on her time with *The Jeffersons* as "all of the cast members got along well on the set; it takes a group of people, a collaborative effort, of which all of these people were a part, that made *The Jeffersons* set run smoothly".

Paula Edelstein - Assistant Associate Producer

Paula Edelstein began as receptionist in 1975 and went on to become an Assistant Associate Producer. She worked with *The Jeffersons* for seven years and "loved every minute." She was nice enough to send me a Jeffersons cast picture from the early 1980s.

Her duties as a receptionist were vast and varied. She was available to the writers, producers, and any teachers on the set. She answered phones, chased people down, and was generally extremely busy.

When the whole cast flew to Hawaii for a special screening of *The Jeffersons*, Edelstein's duties included booking all flights (first class for principals) and rooms (big suites, little suites), arranging per diem and arranging transportation to and from the airports. She kept track of everyone's luggage, and made sure people were present when and where expected. Making sure everyone was satisfied always is a good way to put the essence of Ms. Edelstein's duties. In this case, the trip was worth all the effort. She loved her time in Hawaii, she got to meet "Famous Amos" the Chocolate Chip cookie man. Wally Amos lives in Hawaii, has a company there, and was a guest on the show and the cast were invited to spend time at his home.

Paula noted that *The Jeffersons* did two shows a week. They read on Tuesday, did a run-through on Wednesday, on Thursday there was a full run-through and on Friday there were two tapings, one at 5:30 p.m. and the second at 8:00 p.m. The lot at the time was Tandem Lot (now Metro Media) and shows like *Diff'rent Strokes* and *Sanford and Son* were filmed on the same lot. *The Jeffersons* stage was right next to the *Good Times* stage, which was also a Norman Lear production and Edelstein got a chance to meet many guest stars, such as Brad Pitt, Leonardo DiCaprio, and she even met Jessie Jackson who had been an audience member. Edelstein remembers the cancellation was sad for all as they had worked together for so many years.

Michael S. Baser – Writer

Per my 2019 email interview with writer Michael S. Baser regarding the episode "Once a Friend":

"Elva... Nice to hear you are writing a "Jeffersons" tome. Regarding "Once a Friend", *The Jeffersons* episode I wrote, this episode had an interesting genesis. It was the first ever network show that dealt with transgender issues and (still after all these years) I'm pretty proud of it." The episode was a WGA Award Nominee and would not be repeated for at least the next 10 years. Baser worked with Lear at Tandem TAT for almost eight years.

While we were discussing this show, Baser suggested I contact Michael Moye, who was a college student at the time and had won a Norman Lear scriptwriting contest. Mr. Baser was Moye's guide when he was made a part of Lear's team. Baser and his partner Weiskopf decided to pull a fast one and they gave Moye something to do thinking Moye would not be able to do it. "Well, to make a long story short, not only did Moye deliver, he went on to become a valuable asset to *The Jeffersons* after which he went on to write for *Married with Children* and helped that show become quite successful."

Michael G. Moye - Writer

In my email interview with Mr. Moye, he wrote:

"As I recall, most of the interactions I had with the cast I would deem as cordial. By the time I arrived (Season Five), they had pretty much 'jelled' into the family America loved to visit every Sunday night. Speaking to one was speaking to all. There were very few surprises. Perhaps, the most interesting aspect, especially in light of today's celebrity driven culture, was how truly down to earth they were. If it weren't for all the lights and cameras, it would really feel like we were in George Jefferson's living room."

David Lee - Writer

Lee co-produced a total of 46 episodes from Seasons Ten and Eleven with Peter Casey and 29 episodes as writer/story/teleplay contributor (Seasons Five and Eleven). He and Peter met at Mimeograph in the 70s. After wandering around looking for something to write about and almost getting a shot with the TV sitcom Rhoda, they submitted their "Barney Miller" script to *The Jeffersons*.

They liked the script. (They sold a script to *The Jeffersons* on the day of the Harvey Milk assassination). They wrote their first script about Florence and a religious guy - half of what they wrote stayed in. Mr. Lee was ecstatic, thinking to himself "I'm on my way!" But found out he had to keep his "day job for a while."

He and Mr. Casey "joined the staff a couple of months later." Lee was story editor for six years. They worked with Michael Moye. This turned out to be a "great entry level job, though he did not have a voice about his own personality." Buffoonery was expected and he was not really able to get with it. He did meet Mr. Lear, once. He and his partner "wrote together line by line." They asked questions about what was off-limits. There was no friction. The two writers never ran the show, as in "what themes." They wrote about "social issues and as the show aged issues were exhausted, and episodes were just comfortable, and more family based." Asked if he thought *The Jeffersons* changed TV, Mr. Lee replied, "Oh yeah, a Black family as center of the show, with no struggles and an interracial marriage?" He noted also that the show lasted eleven seasons. Unfortunately, their last episode was not so good. They had no more good ideas and knew they were not coming back after the "Off-Off-Off-Broadway" episode in 1985. He learned a valuable lesson in how to get along with others but felt that he "needed" to do "something else more fulfilling".

Regarding Sherman Hemsley, Mr. Lee thought of him as "quiet, sweet and passive, a great guy, instinctually a character when the camera was on." He thought of Isabel Sanford as a "sweet, dear, kind lady." He admired Marla Gibbs saying she was funny, and as a "business-woman in life was returning her fortune." He hung out with Roxie Roker (said he remembered Lenny Kravitz, Ms. Roker's real-life son) and Cover and Paul Benedict. For David Lee his time with *The Jeffersons* was quite satisfactory.

Ernest Harden, Jr. - Actor

In my interview with Harden, we discussed the fact that his first appearance on *The Jeffersons* was as the character Jason King. After this first appearance Harden was "instrumental in the name change on the script" (from Jason King to Marcus Garvey Henderson) and "was happy to note that the change appeared on every page after his first appearance." The character was so well thought of that Mr. Harden "didn't even have to do a screen test." He was, nonetheless, "nervous as this was a major show" so he wanted to do the best he could. He appreciated the fact that *The Jeffersons* was a "cutting edge" show in that it was dealing with relevant societal issues such as morals and honesty which is why his first appearance as George's helper has him getting caught stealing a jacket from George's cleaning establishment. Mr. Harden "loved" working on *The Jeffersons*. Harden also appeared in big screen movies including *Three Days of the Condor* (1975) and *White Men Can't Jump* (1992), and TV movies including *Roots: The Gift* (1988) and *Intimate Betrayal* (1999). He also appeared in many TV series including *Santa Barbara* (1984), *Atlanta Child Murders* (1985), *Hill Street Blues* (1986), *ER* (2001), *The Parkers* (2001), to name a few and I could go on and on through 2021.

Lydia Nichole - Actor

In answer to an email question from me, I received the following note from Nichole:

"I had the best time working on *The Jeffersons*. The cast was great to me, especially Sherman Hemsley. The show was the number one show at the time, and everyone was wonderful and welcoming to me. "In the second part of "The Strays", I was able to see the power of the stars at work. The producers decided my character should not give George Jefferson a hug and Marla Gibbs, Isabel Stanford and Sherman jumped in and said my character needed to keep that hug because it humanizes the character. The producers backed down and tried to put it on me. They told me to go with what felt right to me. I went with the hug."

Ernest L. Thomas - Actor

I received a lovely note from Mr. Thomas after asking him to share about his experience on *The Jeffersons*:

He wrote: "Sure, I'd be happy to. Being cast as "Train" in *The Jeffersons* was a dream come true for me, it was Heaven on Earth. I remember taking the bus to the audition from this run-down Hotel in Hollywood and I remember the producers were really nice and one of them was really funny and he was a good actor. He read the script with me. When I got to the hotel they said I had gotten the role so I was yelling to the top of my lungs and then the neighbors in the rooms next door started banging on the walls and telling me to shut up. I took the bus there my first day, but Isabel Sanford asked if I needed a ride and I said I can take the bus. But she insisted that she would take me home and pick me up every day for that week. I will never forget her kindness.

I remember the first day of rehearsal I was so nervous but also anxious to show the gift God has given me and the director took me around the table to meet everyone. I had already met Isabel Sanford, but I shook Damon Evan's hand and the great Robert Guillaume, but when they brought me to Sherman Hemsley he wouldn't take my hand, he kind of looked at my hand and said, "Ernest Thomas and so what."

Initially I was hurt but it actually helped me because I wanted to impress him even more. The director and cast members loved my performance but Sherman never said anything the entire week. Come show time I was on fire, the audience loved me and especially the scenes with Sherman and me. I got loud applause at curtain call, but the announcer said "Ernest Thompson" and then Sherman ran out and corrected the announcer and said, "NO his name is Ernest Thomas and he's going to be a star." All of a sudden, he treated me like we were close friends. He told me that I will get my own show but warned me to stay away from people because they're energy vampires and even some close friends would be jealous. He kept repeating stay to yourself and avoid energy vampires. Being on *The Jeffersons* will always hold a special place in my heart."

Jay Hammer – Actor

It took a little time, but I was able to finally locate Mr. Hammer online through his wife. Here is his emailed interview which I deeply appreciated:

"How I was chosen - There was another actor who played Alan Willis first, Andrew Rubin, for one episode. They asked him to come back and he declined. My agent asked me if I would audition to play a black person. I said sure. The audition lasted 3 months of being seen and called back. No screen test and finally given the job.

Progress as an actor – The part was incredibly helpful in my progress as an actor. Working in front of a live audience, 3 cameras and working with such a tremendous cast, writers, and directors.

All of them were wonderfully welcoming to me. I was the first character to join the cast in 5 years and they all couldn't have been more helpful and kind. Minnesota – I didn't even know I went to Minnesota!! I thought I went on a ski trip that I never came back from. And the show continued to run for 6 more years without missing Alan!!

PS FUN FACT: Except for one show with tuxedo – all the clothes I wore were my personal clothes. From Jay April 21, 2019."

Renn Woods - Actor

I was able to catch up with Renn Woods, actor, vocalist, author, and songwriter who remains quite busy with her career. Prior to being on *The Jeffersons*, she had appeared in *Hair, The Jerk, 9 to 5, Car Wash, Sparkle, Roots* and as Dorothy in the first national Broadway tour of *The Wiz*. When asked about being chosen for her role on this *Jeffersons* episode and whether she was nervous or not, seeing that she was already successful in her career, Ms. Woods says she was thrilled to be there, not nervous. She found it monumental that there was a show that portrayed successful Black people. Her part started out as Florence's sister but was changed to her cousin. Ms. Woods also did have one little problem in that she wanted to appear "as is", meaning without wearing a wig. However, the powers that be were not in favor of dreadlocks and so on went a wig. Ms. Woods told me that she found Norman Lear to be brutally honest which is a trait she admires. Her appearance helped give a boost to her career for which she is appreciative.

Willie Tyler - Actor – Ventriloquist
Lester couldn't make it

Mr. Tyler and I were able to have a nice long chat via the phone: He talked about how he came to appear on *The Jeffersons* and about how he became a ventriloquist.

At the age of ten while living in Detroit, Willie saw the ventriloquist Paul Winchell with his dummy Jerry Mahoney on television. Willie immediately decided he wanted to emulate this man. He began practicing a lot with his sister's doll. He eventually found a lady who made his first small dummy "Lester" (named by Willie's brother), and both his medium and bigger Lester, the one he currently uses most of the time.

Tyler saw an advertisement for ventriloquist classes in *Popular Mechanics*. A teacher helped him enroll. He would later use his talents to entertain his fellow Air Force recruits. When he returned to his hometown of Detroit, he joined the up-and-coming Motown record label. Before getting the gig on *The Jeffersons*, Willie had made a name for himself working and touring with Motown for eight years, recording an album "Hello Dummy" and appearing in various nightclubs. He performed at the Apollo and at first was "losing, losing and finally started winning and enjoyed it."

He and Lester were the emcees for the Motown Revue when it toured. When Motown performers like The Supremes and Temptations grew more famous, Tyler and Lester were the opening act. Tyler worked with Sinatra, and Sammy Davis, Jr. and opened for the last Diana Ross and the Supremes Act in Las Vegas in 1970. When Tyler began working with Motown, the Lester he used was the third and last version of the doll. The third Lester was much larger, and easier for the audiences in the balconies to see. Lester got an Afro in 1978. They both appeared on the *Letterman* show and did McDonald's commercials.

Willie had written numerous times to the casting people for a chance to appear on *The Jeffersons* and he finally heard from them. He had a meeting with the writers (he cancelled an appointment with Andy Williams), and they liked his treatment of the character they were looking for. The character he was hired to play, Ray Crandall, had been in a mental institution, and, of course, this provided fodder for insults from George and funny lines from others in the cast. The "message" this episode was supposed to convey was that people with mental illnesses were not all "raving lunatics". Willie told me that during his appearance, he was mostly "in the moment" and concerned with whether he would get his lines right and that this appearance helped his career. Willie thought that Sherman Hemsley was a "quiet guy." He says he was pleasantly surprised when he saw that the show was classy.

Steve Devorkin – Actor

In 2019, late summer, I was able to interview Steve Devorkin who played the part of Wilbur the Whistling Gnome. Steve wore a gnome outfit over the top of his body and his real bellybutton whistled the tune "Sweet Georgia Brown". He found out about the part through one of the new writers on the show. They told him the show was looking for an overweight, small actor with a big belly. Steve was not exactly happy about his size, but at least it could land him a part. He auditioned and got the part. Steve says he chose "Sweet Georgia Brown" as his whistling song because "it had gone out of copyright." During taping he received good advice from one of the principals, Paul Benedict, who told him to "always be on" and "business-like" because the tapes were always rolling. Working with *The Jeffersons* cast was new and exciting and comfortable for Steve (due to his large ego at the time, he knew that he was "supposed to be there" and that he was "one call away" from stardom). Devorkin detected some discomfort among the cast members regarding whether *The Jeffersons* would be picked up the next season. This possibility had no effect on Devorkin as he was very sure of his own path to stardom. He had one other joyous happening that night of the taping: Devorkin's wife gave birth to a son.

Ralph Leon Davis
Camera Utility

Mr. Davis worked as Camera Utility person off and on for ten years on *The Jeffersons*, *AITF*, *Maude*, and *Good Times*. He attended Loyola Marymount in Los Angeles and due to being in the right place at the right time he began his career as a Page, an entry level position at Metro Media. He worked with the *Soul Train* television dance program, meeting and greeting guests while working as Camera Assistant on *Soul Train* and with the Norman Lear sitcoms. Mr. Davis informed me that working with *The Jeffersons* was "one of the best experiences" he has had, that the cast was "one of the best, down to earth, close-knit groups" with whom he has worked. He was "impressed" with *The Jeffersons* as it was "ground-breaking." The show employed the first Black Directors, Tony Singletary and Arlando Smith, and the first Black female Boom Operator, Phyllis Bailey Brooks. Mr. Davis remains friends with the show's producer.

Chapter Nineteen:
Behind the Scenes

Along with cast members, producers, and those wonderful writers, there are certain other essential persons without which a show could not have much chance of reaching the top. I was not able to locate and interview all the crew members who worked on *The Jeffersons* but with the help of the Jeffersons staff I was able to garner a bit of information about some of those who were instrumental in helping to make *The Jeffersons* successful. I apologize to those not mentioned as part of this group of people. I have used these people as representatives of those behind-the-scenes workers who deserve kudos for the hard work and perseverance that went into the making of one of the highest-rated television sitcoms of all time.

Adella Farmer - Costume Designer. Her career would take her to the set of *Good Times* (where she chose Esther Rolle's wardrobe), *227* and other venues.

Arlando Smith - Director. He was also an Emmy and Luminas Awards winner.

Betsey Potter - Costume Designer. She would go on to garner four Daytime Emmy Nominations and two Prime Time Emmy nominations.

Billie Jordan - Make-up Artist. She held this position from 1978-1985.

Donald A. Morgan - Cinematographer from 1978-1981. Went on to win nine Prime Time Emmy Awards.

Don Rosemond - Property Master.

Donna Marcione Pollack - Costume Designer. Has since worked on films such as *Star Trek Into Darkness*.

Karen Edwards - Hair Stylist. Has gone on to work on movies such as *The Phantom of the Opera* (2004) and *I'll Find You* (2019).

Paula Edelstein - Began as the Receptionist for Norman Lear and *The Jeffersons* cast and crew; in my opinion, one of the most important positions on the set. She has worked many years in the entertainment industry with major producers, entertainment companies and broadcast journalists. She is a writer and freelance journalist. She has received the Editor's Choice Award from the International Library of Poetry. Ms. Edelstein is now a licensed realtor/broker and owns her own firm. **(See Interview with Paula Edelstein - Chapter Eighteen)**

Phyllis Bailey Brooks - First Black Female Boom Operator on a network show. Having progressed in her acting and singing endeavors Ms. Brooks has allowed herself to be available for a quote for this book in answer to a question from me regarding the cast photo in this book: "It's wonderful that you are doing this! Yes, that's me! I started on the show as a Page with Paula, then cable puller, then promoted a couple of seasons later as the first Black woman Boom Operator on a network show. I was on the show for at least eight years. I was also on all of Lear's shows of the day, holding it down as an aspiring actor/vocalist looking to find a way to be a part of my awesome art media community."

Ralph Leon Davis - Camera Utility. **(See Interview with Ralph Leon Davis - Chapter Eighteen)**

Ray Hall - Hair Stylist from 1975-1985. Discovered in a Sunset Boulevard Salon by actor Berlinda Tolbert who was so pleased with Ray's hair styling skills she recommended him, incessantly, to the bosses until he was hired.

Rene Williams - Make-up Artist. She was make-up artist for 161 episodes.

Rita Riggs - Costume Designer. Her work on shows like *Divorce American Style* led to her work on *All in the Family*, which led to *Maude, Sanford and Son, Good Times, One Day at a Time,* and *Mary Hartman, Mary Hartman*. Fun Fact: To create the wardrobe for Isabel Sanford in *The Jeffersons*, Riggs went to New York, walked down the street where the Louise Jefferson character lived, around the block past the dress shops that she would be walking by and imagined what the character would buy. In 2003, Riggs received the Career Achievement Award in Television from the Costume Designers Guild Awards. She was also acknowledged at the 2018 Oscars "In Memoriam" for her work as a Costume Designer in Hollywood.

Stu Rudolph - Camera Assistant.

Tony Singletary - Director. His directorial skills were instrumental in many television sitcoms, including *One Day at a Time, Charles in Charge, The Redd Foxx Show, 227, Who's the Boss? Martin, Hangin' with Mr. Cooper*, and the list goes on.

Chapter Twenty:
Awards and Nominations

Golden Globes, USA 1985
Nominee
Golden Globe
Best Television Series - Comedy or Musical
Best Performance by an Actress in a Television Series - Comedy or Musical
Isabel Sanford
Best Performance by an Actor in a Television Series - Comedy or Musical
Sherman Hemsley
Best Performance by an Actress in a Supporting Role in a Series, Miniseries or Motion Picture Made for Television
Marla Gibbs

Golden Globes, USA 1984
Nominee
Golden Globe
Best Performance by an Actress in a Television Series - Comedy or Musical
Isabel Sanford

Golden Globes, USA 1983
Nominee
Golden Globe
Best Performance by an Actress in a Television Series - Comedy or Musical
Isabel Sanford

Golden Globes, USA 1978
Nominee
Golden Globe
Best Actress in a Television Series - Comedy or Musical
Isabel Sanford

Golden Globes, USA 1977
Nominee
Golden Globe
Best Actress in a Television Series - Comedy or Musical
Isabel Sanford

Primetime Emmy Awards 1985
Nominee
Primetime Emmy
Outstanding Lead Actress in a Comedy Series
Isabel Sanford
For playing "Louise Jefferson"
Outstanding Supporting Actress in a Comedy Series
Marla Gibbs
For playing "Florence Johnston"

Primetime Emmy Awards 1984
Nominee
Primetime Emmy
Outstanding Lead Actor in a Comedy Series
Sherman Hemsley
For playing "George Jefferson"
Outstanding Lead Actress in a Comedy Series
Isabel Sanford
For playing "Louise Jefferson"
Outstanding Supporting Actress in a Comedy Series
Marla Gibbs
For playing "Florence Johnston"

Primetime Emmy Awards 1983
Winner
Primetime Emmy
Outstanding Video Tape Editing for a Series
Larry Harris
For episode "Change of a Dollar"
Nominee
Primetime Emmy
Outstanding Lead Actress in a Comedy Series
Isabel Sanford
For playing "Louise Jefferson"
Outstanding Supporting Actress in a Comedy, Variety or Music Series
Marla Gibbs
For playing "Florence Johnston"

Primetime Emmy Awards 1982
Nominee
Primetime Emmy
Outstanding Lead Actress in a Comedy Series
Isabel Sanford
For playing: "Louise Jefferson"
Outstanding Supporting Actress in a Comedy or Variety or Music Series
Marla Gibbs
For playing: "Florence Johnston"

Primetime Emmy Awards 1981
Winner
Primetime Emmy
Outstanding Lead Actress in a Comedy Series
Isabel Sanford
For playing "Louise Jefferson"
Nominee
Primetime Emmy
Outstanding Supporting Actress in a Comedy or Variety or Music Series

Marla Gibbs
For playing "Florence Johnston"

Primetime Emmy Awards 1980
Nominee
Outstanding Lead Actress in a Comedy Series
Isabel Sanford
For playing "Louise Jefferson"

Primetime Emmy Awards 1979
Nominee
Outstanding Lead Actress in a Comedy Series
Isabel Sanford
For playing: "Louise Jefferson"

Humanitas Prize 1978
Nominee
Humanitas Prize
30 Minute Network or Syndicated Television
Roger Shulman
John Baskin
For *The Jeffersons*: 984 W. 124th Street, Apt. 5C (1977)

Image Awards (NAACP) 1982
Winner
Image Award
Best Performance by an Actor in a Comedy Series or Special
Sherman Hemsley
Best Performance by an Actress in a Comedy Series or Special
Marla Gibbs

TV Land Awards 2008
Nominee
TV Land Award
Neighbor You Try to Avoid
Paul Benedict

TV Land Awards 2006
Nominee
TV Land Award
Favorite Made-for-TV Maid
Marla Gibbs

TV Land Awards 2005
Nominee
TV Land Award
Favorite Mother-In-Law
Zara Cully
Favorite Nosy Neighbor
Paul Benedict

TV Land Awards 2004
Winner
TV Land Award
Favorite Cantankerous Couple
Sherman Hemsley
Isabel Sanford
Nominee
TV Land Award
Favorite Made-for-TV Maid
Marla Gibbs
Favorite "Big, Bad Momma"
Zara Cully

TV Land Awards 2003
Nominee
TV Land Award
Comedy Theme Song You Can't Get Out of Your Head
Most Memorable Male Guest Star in a Comedy as Himself
Billy Dee Williams

Writers Guild of America, USA 1978
Nominee
WGA Award (TV)

Episodic Comedy
Michael S. Baser
Kim Weiskopf
For *The Jeffersons*: Once a Friend (1977)

Young Artist Awards 1985
Nominee
Young Artist Award
Best Young Actor - Guest in a Television Series
Jaleel White

Chapter Twenty-One:
Production Credits

Norman Lear	Creator/ Producer
Sylvia Ogilvie	Assistant to Producer
David W. Duclon	Executive Producer
Ron Leavitt	Creative Consultant
Jerry Perzigian	Executive Producer
Jay Moriarty	Executive Producer
Mike Milligan	Executive Producer
Don Nicholl	Executive Producer
Michael Ross	Executive Producer
George Sunga	Associate Producer
Bernie West	Executive Producer
Michael G. Moye	Executive Producer
Don Seigel	Executive Producer
Ron Leavitt	Executive Producer
Peter Casey	Producer
David Lee	Producer
Jack Shea	Producer
Sy Rosen	Producer
Sylvia O'Gilvie	Associate Producer
Ken Stump	Associate Producer
Tedd Anasti	Associate Producer
Arlando Smith	Director
Tony Singletary	Director
Jane Murray	Principal Casting Executive
Sara Finney-Johnson	Program Consultant / Production Associate
Alan Horn	Production Supervisor
Bob Lally	Assistant Director
Karen C. Miller	Production Associate

Leon Euslander Lighting Director
Don Roberts Series Art Director

Composer: Theme music
Ja'net DuBois & Jeff Barry

Singer: Theme music
Ja'net DuBois

PRODUCTION LOCATION(S)
CBS Television City, Hollywood, California (1975)
Metromedia Square, Hollywood, California
(1975–1982)
Universal City Studios, Universal City, California
(1982–1985)
Camera setup
Multi-camera
Running time
22–24 minutes
Production company(s)
T.A.T. Communications Company
(1975–1982)
(Seasons 1-8)
NRW Productions
(1975–1979)
(Seasons 1-5)
Ragamuffin Productions
(1980–1981)
(Season 7)
Embassy Television
(1982–1985)
(Seasons 9-11)

Chapter Twenty-Two:
Afterword

By John H. McWhorter, Associate Professor of Linguistics
at Columbia University

I am especially honored, not to mention tickled, that Elva Green asked me to write this afterword. Just by chance, it was my pandemic project to finally rewatch the whole eleven-season run of *The Jeffersons*.

It was a key part of my television heritage, as a black kid who grew up watching a lot of television in the 1970s. *The Jeffersons* premiered when I was nine, and I remember watching the first episode and knowing it would be one of my must-watch shows from then on. It was, for several years, and just the thought of Isabel Sanford, in that smoky baritone of hers, beaming and reaching out for Hemsley and exclaiming "Oh, George ...!" will forever remind me of being a kid with no problems.

When it was quietly cancelled ten years later in 1985, I doubt I was alone in having not known the show was even still running. I had gone away to college and stopped watching much TV (temporarily, of course!). One heard that Lionel and Jenny split up at the end – but what else? Since the DVD era began I have always had it in the back of mind to find out, and watching all 253 episodes forty years on has been a trip indeed in all senses of the word. *The Jeffersons* wasn't as deep as it seemed to me when I was a kid, when adults having problems, alone, looked "serious." But I will always love this show to pieces.

What stands out almost fifty years after the premiere is what a treasure Sherman Hemsley's performance was. The bantam brawler he created – and Hemsley was nothing like him in real life – was a kind of symbol of Black America after the Civil Rights victories of the 1950s and 1960s, proudly savoring his success, knowing full well what color he was, and under no impression that White was better (unless he needed to imitate it for pragmatic purposes). It was fairly brilliant that you never tire of the character over so very many episodes. In interviews later, Hemsley claimed that he required the writers to soften how George treated Mr. Bentley and Tom Willis, but if this happened it was only slightly. George is himself to the end, and I think we all liked him that way. He was our avatar.

Yet the truly forever performance on the show was Marla Gibbs' Florence. There was more to her than funny putdowns of George. Gibbs accomplished so much without yelling, managing something that today Wanda Sykes pulls off similarly: punch with economy. Any black person has an aunt or a cousin who talks and acts like Florence, and her depiction as church-going lady makes her even realer. A different Florence could easily have been written as a kind of good-time girl on her nights off – *ha ha* – but making Florence a "home girl" was a nice touch.

And there was a little more. If one is to engage 253 episodes of anything, it's the chords, the underlying harmonies, or what I might go too far and call the subtexts, that are interesting, and *The Jeffersons* was full of them.

One: underneath Florence's knocks on George rang a bit of "You may be rich, but you're still black," as in, subordinated by larger society. It wasn't that Hemsley's George actually needed this putdown; he was so black-positive that he hardly needed to be reminded of where he came from. But in an early episode after the main characters have been brawling messily for 10 minutes, Florence stands chewing gum with a dismissive look conveying, "Y'all may have money but …" The audience – with a goodly proportion of black Los Angelenos, just as on *Sanford & Son* at the same time -- howls for half a minute and anyone black watching knew why. The reason George put up with Florence's putdowns was a sense that she was ultimately signalling that blackness was their common condition.

Another subtext, which will require first a bit of delicate throat-clearing. The show was modern for its era in how often references are made, albeit politely, to George and Louise having a sex life. However, as real as Hemsley and Sanford seemed as a couple overall, if I may, I compare, for example, the real chemistry that Della Reese and Redd Foxx created on the short-lived *The Royal Family* in the early 90s. We never truly saw that sort of connection between George and Weezy, any more than you saw it between Bea Arthur and Bill Macy on *Maude* despite their similar references to what went on upstairs.

As such, in a way, the real sex on *The Jeffersons* was in the endless battle of wits between George and Florence (just as one might suppose, as a skit on *In Living Color* had it, that the real love match on *Sanford & Son* was between Fred and Aunt Esther). Neither was ever either lastingly hurt or truly bested; rather, the wit-fest was a kind of affectionate callisthenic in disguise.

Or, a little more subtext: twice we got a look at how well Hemsley and Roxie Roker as Helen danced together. Their characters didn't like each other much. But when it came to moving to music, Hemsley and Roker became the seasoned musical performers that both were, temporarily making you forget that they were supposed to be married to Weezy and Tom respectively. For all of the big news that the Willises being interracial was at the time, back then it was easy for producers to be so caught up in the progressiveness of the gesture that they forgot to cast for chemistry. It isn't an accident that the one episode that features mostly the Willises alone – stranded in an unexpectedly tacky hotel room late in Season Ten – doesn't work, because we don't really believe them as soul mates. What we do believe is Hemsley and Roker when they dance – on another show they could have played a couple.

Overall, *The Jeffersons* is also fun in how many "Whodathunkits" it entailed in real life. It would never have occurred to me that Sanford was 21 years older than Hemsley, to the point that you almost imagine him calling her "Mrs. Sanford" when they first met. That two people with such an age difference seemed so plausible as a couple was rather marvelous, and "Black Don't Crack" was only part of it. (There was a similar age difference between Esther Rolle and John Amos on *Good Times*.) One was always struck by the fact that both Lionels had the same last name, Evans, but few know that Michael Evans and Berlinda Tolbert were born a day apart and in the same state (North Carolina). Paul Benedict, as Bentley, was not British but American.

Or, for all of the resonance that Zara Cully's Mother Jefferson justly created—Cully resonated as strongly as Hemsley and Gibbs and the character remains one of the most interesting mothers-in-law in television's history -- she actually was only on the show for a few seasons before she passed away. On Cully, it was a (racist) scandal that white Judith Lowry, playing an octogenarian on *Phyllis* at the same time, got major press for working at her age when Cully was 1) only two years younger and 2) just plain better than Lowry.

The Jeffersons rarely cut as deeply as Norman Lear's other shows like *All in the Family* and *Maude* tried to. There were no facelifts or abortions; no one was killed. There were indeed Very Special episodes such as the one where George runs up against Ku Klux Klan members. But there were more episodes reminding us that, fundamentally, the show was just a generation past *I Love Lucy*. This was especially so as time passed, with 70s-sitcom staples such as the spell in jail with prostitutes, getting stuck in a backwoods cabin, and the time when everybody goes to Hawaii.

Yet for all of that, for black viewers the show was heritage, plain and simple. Revisiting it has been, I say almost sincerely, a religious experience. I will never forget making a reference to the show during my first month or so of college, when a white guy instantly dismissed the whole show as trivial nonsense. I was a little hurt, although I could see it through his eyes. *The Jeffersons* was by no means Ibsen (or August Wilson), and only rarely pretended otherwise. But that guy didn't get that it was nevertheless, for us, family.

George calls out Tom and Helen's son for being "mixed" and the two engage in television's first depiction of The Dozens. (This was the first time I heard anyone yell "Yo' Mama!" as George does when bested at the end.) Michael Evans as Lionel, questioning his life path, sings a bit of "Cabaret" at the piano down at Charlie's Bar. A flashback many seasons in has George and Louise establishing the first branch of Jefferson Cleaners in 1968, complete with Sanford perfectly switching back to the more uncoiffed and down-to-earth version of Louise she originated on *All in the Family* and carried into the first season of *The Jeffersons*, before going posher as Louise presumably embraced her new income bracket. Mother Jefferson and Harry Bentley doing The Bump -- there's a reason a still of that gets around so much.

Of the hot black sitcom hits of the 1970s, *The Jeffersons*, in its way, just wins. *Sanford and Son* was delightful, but fundamentally just sad, with the actors' spray-grayed hair and the studiously junky clutter of the set. *Good Times* was a gloomy business, too, and also never really made much sense. There was the J.J. problem–*he* was a ladies' man and a good painter? – which in addition lost the show John Amos and kept Rolle away for a long spell.

The Jeffersons, churning gamely with no major cast changes (except the Lionel thing) and no off-screen conflicts through its endless run, evidently selling enough soap to make wary execs leave it alone, ran about as long as *Sanford and Son* and *Good Times* combined, and was an actual Good Time as well. Legend has *The Cosby Show* introducing America to black affluence on television, but *The Jeffersons* had done that job almost a decade before. Showing what it could be like to Move On Up for ten years-plus, *The Jeffersons* just *was*. And today, with a little patience and nostalgia, we see that it still *is*.

Index

Numbers in **bold** indicate photographs

227 126, 136, 139, 154, 156
"984 W. 124th St, Apt. 5C" 57, 62, 160

Abbott, Mea 41
Acosta, Dorothy 138
Adlon, Pamela 128
"Agreement, The" 48, 53
Aidekman, Al 121, 129
Akers, Susann 122
Albrecht, Howard 47, 57, 67
Albright, Frankie 114
Alfasa, Joe 87
"All I Want for Christmas" 96
All in the Family 1, 2-3, 4, 5-6, 7-8, 9-11, 12, 13, 14, 18, 19, 21, 23, 30, 42, **73**, **74**, 125, 138, 141, 152, 155, 168
Alldredge, Michael 55
Allen, Raymond 67
Allen, Ta-Ronce 97
"Alley Oops" 97
Ames, Leon 39
Amos, John 167, 169
Amos, Wally 95, 99, 145
Anasti, Tedd 47, 163
"Anatomy of a Stain" 110
"And the Doorknobs Shined Like Diamonds" 97, 99-100
"And the Winner Is…" 121
"And Up We Go" 130
Anderson, John 98
Anderson, Marilyn 113
Andrews, Roy 98
Androsky, Carole 28
Angelle, Bobby 97
"Announcement, The" 87, 91-92
"Appointment in 8-B" 112
Ari, Bob 114
"Arrival, Pt. 1, The" 89
"Arrival, Pt. 2, The" 89
"As Florence Turns" 96, 99
Ashby, John 29, 39, 49
A-Team, The 116, 124, 131
Atkinson, Bruce 95
Auberjonois, Rene 39
Avalos, Luis 88
Avery, James 122, 124

"Baby Love" 88
Baer, Art 28
Baker, Jack 58
Ball, Fred 95
Balmagia, Larry 50
Banks, Ernie Lee 28, 121
Barlow, Jennifer 131
Barney Miller 146
Baron, Millie 128
Barra, Vanda 112
Barrett, Clyde J. 106
Barry, Jeff 25, 164
Barselou, Paul 48, 56
Baser, Michael S. viii, 55, 60, 146, 162
Baskin, John 27, 55, 56, 57, 58, 62, 160
Bass, Emory 68

Baublitz, Bob 48, 66, 67, 90
Bay, Frances 97
Beard, Matthew (Stymie) 87
Beck, Billy 130
"Bedtime Story, A" 67
Begal, Cindy 97
Belous, Paul M. 48, 50, 57, 59, 65, 67, 68, 88
Beltran, Alma 68
Bendetson, Bob and Howard 95, 96, 102
Benedict, Paul v, 11, 19-20, 24, 26, **74, 76, 77**, 106, 116, 124, 131, 141, 143, 147, 152, 160, 161, 167
Bensfield, Dick 27
"Bentley's Problem" 49
Benton, James Grant 95
Berlinger, Warren 129
Bernard, Jason 120
Bertrand, Alma 58
Best of the Jeffersons, The 139-140
Billings, Earl 98
Birkett, Bernadette 122
Black Panthers, The 10
Black, Gerry 89
"Blackout, The" 58
Blackwell, Tamu 67
Blaisdell, Brad 89
"Blazing Jeffersons" 104
Blevins, Donna 96
"Blood and Money" 127
Blow, Peggy 129
"Bobbles, Bungles, and Boo Boos" 127
"Bodyguards Are People Too" 113
Bogert, William 58, 90
Bonaduce, Anthony and Celia 89, 90
Bonar, Becky 128
Bonnell, Vivian 97
Boroff, Phil 115

Bottoms, John 67
Bovingloh, Don 89
Bowen, Earl 88
Boyer, Peter J. 99
Boyle, Don 40
Brackett-Zika, Christian 122
Bradshaw, Booker 48
Braxton, Robin 121
Braxton, Stephanie 115
"Break-Up, Pt. 1, The" 40
"Break-Up, Pt. 2, The" 41
Bright, Ronnell 27
Brody, Jane 68
Bronder, William 129
Brooks, Phyllis Bailey 153, 155
Brooks, Randy 122
Brosten, Harve 27
"Brother Tom" 89, 93
Brown, Johnny 111, 116, 117
Brown, Julie 121
Brown, Renee 89
Brown, Ruth 98
Brown, Sharon 97
Brown, Tom 40, 67
Browning, Rod 58
Bruns, Philip 98
Bryant, Lee 89
Bryant, William 95, 96
Buck, Jerry 72
Bumatai, Andy 95
Burditt, George 40
Burleigh, Robert 111
Burnham, Ed 122
Burns, Joseph 59
Burrell, Deborah 121
Bush, Grand L. 112
Bush, Sherry 95
Butts, Dorothy 39, 43, 88, 121, 127
Byrde, Edye 67
Byron, Jean 98

Cadogan, Alice 123
"Calendar Girl" 96
Call, Ed 123
Callegari, Kim 97
Calloway, Thomas 110
Calvert, Bill 87
Calvert, James 87
Cambridge, Ed 48
Campise, Jeanne 89
"Camp-Out, The" 56
Carlson, Dr. Stan 96
Carlson, Jim 28
Carney, Fred 130
Carry III, Julius 131
Carson, Barbara 49
Carson, Darwyn 121
Carter, John Dewey 115, 123
Carter, T. K. 65
Carter, Terry 104
"Case of Black and White, A" 49
"Case of Self-Defense, A" 105
Case, Tom 104
Casey, Peter 67, 88, 89, 90, 96, 97, 102, 103, 104, 105, 106, 110, 111, 112, 114, 115, 121, 122, 124, 129, 130, 131, 146-147, 163
Castillo, Gerald 58, 68
Cervantes, Gary Carlos 97
"Chairman of the Bored, The" 129, 134
"Change of a Dollar" 114, 118-119, 159
Charisse, Zan 96
Charles, Gloria 127
"Charlie's Angels" 111
"Charmed Life, A" 104
Charo vi, 128, 132, 133
Checking In 98, 101
Childress, Alvin 28, 32, 57
Christiansen, Roseanna 102, 103
"Christmas Wedding, The" 48-49

Chung, Caleb 87
Chung, Esmond 95, 96
Clark, Oliver 131
Clarke, Hope 57
Clarkson, Lana 121
Clayton, Jeffrey 97
Clement, Gertrude 128
Cleveland, Patience 130
Colbin, Rod 55
Coleman, Gary vi, 58
Collings, Patrick 88
Collins, Patrick 87, 98
Colognne, Bernadette 105
"Command Post, The" 122
Conforti, Gino 88, 127
Conley, Darlene 68
Connell, Gordon 65, 88
Considine, John 121
Cooke, Victoria 129
Cooper, Ilene 114, 115
Cooper, Zackie 38
Cosby Show, The 131, 169
"Costume Party, The" 57
Cover, Franklin 11, 16-17, 24, 26, 72, **74**, **76**, **77**, **80**, **86**, 93, 116, 131, 136, 139, 141, 142, 147
Cozens, Mimi 88
Craig, Carl M. 124
Crouch, Andrae vi, 105, 108
Cruickshanks, Reid 96
Culler, Sip 67
Cully, Zara v, 10, 11, 17, 24, 26, 36, 51, 53, 56, 62-63, **76**, **77**, **85**, 142, 161, 168
Cunningham, Rhonda 51
Curtis, Keene 42
Dale, Ted 57, 65, 102
Dallas 96, 99
Darlow, Linda 127
Dart, Irene 90
"Date with Danger, A" 111

Davalos, Richard 89
Davenport, Bill 49
Davis, Herb 66
Davis, Jr., Sammy vi, 43-44, 122, 124, 125, 151
Davis, Ralph Leon 152-153, 155
De Vol, Frank 97, 100, 104, 105
De'Amore, JoJo 96
Dean, James F. 128
"Death Smiles on a Dry Cleaner, Pt. 1" 111-112
"Death Smiles on a Dry Cleaner, Pt. 2" 112
Deems, Mickey 48
DeFazio, Sam 89
"Defiant Ones, The" 113
Del Mar, Marcia 127
Del Regno, John 114
DeLano, Michael 97
Delegall, Bob 102
Dendy, LaShanda 97
Dent, Frank 103
"Designing Woman" 114-115
DeVinney, Bob 57
Devorkin, Steve viii, 131, 136, 152
Dewitt, Fay 56
DiCaprio, Leonardo 145
Diller, Phyllis vi, 128, 133
Dillon, Melinda 39
"Dinner for Harry, A" 38, **77**
"Do Not Forsake Me, Oh My Helen" 106
"Dog-Gone" viii, 104, 107-108
Dolan, Don 104
Donaldson, Norma 40
Donley, John 42, 67
Donovan, Martin 57
Doolittle, Robert 65
DoQui, Robert 48
"Double Trouble" 115
Douglas, Geary 96

Douglas, Ronalda 57, 61
Downey, Dee 13
Downing, Brian 129
Downing, David 68, 111, 112
Drake, Bebe 112
Drake, Michele 129
DuBois, Ja'net 25, **79**, 164
Duclon, David W. 96, 104, 106, 110, 111, 112, 163
Duggan, Bob 48, 95
Dukes, David 47
Dunbar, Olive 104
DuPois, Starletta 89
Duteil, Jeffrey 104

Earlie, Randy 115
"Ebony and Ivory" 127
Eckhaus, Richard B. 58
Edelstein, Paula viii, 145, 155
Edwards, Karen 155
Egan, Patrick 114, 115
Eichen, Cheri 127, 129, 130, 131
Eisenmann, Ike 97
Ellerbee, Bobby F. 58, 59
Emerson, Karrie 105
Epp, Marita 114
Erwin, Bill 111
Euslander, Leon 164
Evans, Damon viii, 21, 26, 42, 52, 57, **76**
Evans, Estelle 39, 43
Evans, Mike 5, 9, 11, 18, 26, 29, 42, 52, **73**, **74**, **75**, 87, 91, 102, 129, 130, 143, 144, 167, 168
"Every Night Fever" 68
"Expectant Father, The" 88

Fann, Al 98
Farmar, Adella **84**, 144, 154
Farr, Gordon 28
Farrel, Sylvia 121

Farrell, Marty 121, 123
"Father Christmas" 122
"Father's Day" 114, 118
Fields, Jere 129
Finney, Sara V. 104, 122, 125, 131
Finney-Johnson, Sara 163
"First and Last Supper, The" 9
"First Store, The" 90-91, 94
Fisher, John 143
Fisher, Robert 39
Flanagan, Neil 89
Fletcher, Jack 58, 121, 123, 127
"Florence Did It Different, Pt. 1"
    103, 106-107
"Florence Did It Different, Pt. 2"
    103, 107
"Florence Gets Lucky" 57
"Florence in Love" 48
"Florence Meets Mr. Right" 67
"Florence's Cousin" 96
"Florence's New Job, Pt. 1" 98, 101
"Florence's New Job, Pt. 2" 98, 101
"Florence's Problem" 41, 45-46
"Florence's Union" 58
"Former Neighbors" 28
Foronjy, Richard 130
Fox, Bernard 111, 112
Fox, Fred S. 41, 49, 66, 98, 103
Fox, Nancy 90
Francis, Ivor vi, 27, 104
Frazier, Joe vi, 128, 133
Freeman, Arny 47
"Freeze-In, The" 69
Freiman, Richard 48, 50, 58
Fresco, David 127
Fresh Prince of Bel-Air, The 124,
    140
Friedman, Lester D. 37
"Friend in Need, A" 27, **80**
Frishman, Daniel 104
Frommer, Ben 110

Fumilayo 58
Furst, Stephen 122

Gagen, Annie 96
Gagen, Tom 96
"Gang's All Here, The" 129-130
Garland, Trish 129
Garrett, Susie 123, 131
Garvey, Marcus 61
Gayle, Rozelle 27, 33
Gedeon, Conroy 122
Gelman, Morrie 2
Gemignani, Rhoda 40
Gendel, Morgan 132, 136
"George and Jimmy" 58
"George and Louise in a Bind, Pt.
    1" 58, 62
"George and Louise in a Bind, Pt.
    2" 59
"George and Louise in a Bind, Pt.
    3" 59
"George and the Manager" 40
"George and the President" 47
"George and Whitty" 57
"George Finds a Father" 67
"George Meets Whittendale" 41
"George Needs Help" 57
"George the Philanthropist" 50
"George vs. Wall Street" 40
"George Who?" 66
"George Won't Talk" 39, 44
"George's Alibi" 40
"George's Best Friend" 40, 44-45
"George's Birthday" 90
"George's Diploma" 47
"George's Dream" 66
"George's Family Tree" 27
"George's First Vacation" 38
"George's Guilt" 49
"George's Help" 55-56, 61
"George's Legacy" 56

"George's New Stockbroker" 66, 71, **81**
"George's Old Girl Friend" 123
"George's Skeleton" 28, 32
Gerken, Ellen 131
"Getting Back to Basiks" 122
Giambalvo, Vito J. 129
Gibbs, Ann 41, 127
Gibbs, Dorian 122
Gibbs, Marla iv, v, viii, 17-18, 24, 26, 29-30, 31, 38, 43, 59, 60, 63-64, 72, **74, 78, 81, 86,** 99, 101, 106-107, 108-109, 125, 128, 131, 132, 136, 139-140, 141, 142, 144, 147, 148, 157, 158, 159-160, 161, 166, 168
Gibbs, Timothy 87
Gibson, Cal 58, 131
Gierasch, Stefan 120
"Gift, The" 128
Gill, Jr., Will 105, 114
Gittlin, Joyce 105, 113, 120, 127
Gjonola, Dick 110
"God Bless Americans" 97
Goldberg, Marshall 96
Goldman, Stu 129
Goldstein, Lew 114, 115, 128
Gonzalez, Santiago 28
"Good Life, The" **81**, 114, 117-118
"Good News, Bad News" 56
Good Times 3, 10, 25, 30, 38, 54, 116, 117, 145, 152, 154, 155, 167, 169
Gorman, Bob 87, 106
Gossett, Jr., Louis 40, 44-45
Gould, Jackie 30
Gourdine, Anthony 89
"Grand Opening, Pt. 1, The" 55
"Grand Opening, Pt. 2, The" 55
Grant, Perry 27
Grant, Sarina C. 98

Green, Eddie 44
Greer, Ingrid 65
Gregory, Sharee 120
Grier, Roosevelt vi, 121, 124
Gries, Jon 120
Grossman, Dixie Brown 28, 40, 48, 49
Grover, Edward 66
Guerdat, Andy 58
Guess Who's Coming to Dinner 8, 13, 109
"Guess Who's Not Coming to Dinner?" 105, 108-109
Guillaume, Robert 39, 44, 149
Guillory, Bennet 121
Gunn, Moses 28, 32

Haden, Stephanie 96
"Hail to the Chief" 130
"Half a Brother" 66
Hall, LaSaundra 105
Hall, Ray 144, 155
Halsey, Michael 122
Hamilton, Kim 113
Hammer, Jay viii, 21, 26, 65, 68, 149-150
Handler, Ruby 121
Hanna, Walt 91
Hanrahan, John V. 50
Hanson, Marcy 129
Harcum, Bob 59
Harden, Jr., Ernest viii, 20, 26, 50, 55-56, 57, 58, 59, 61, 68, 69, **83,** 88, 147-148
Harman, Barry 27
Harrington, Al 95, 96
Harris, Henry 49
Harris, Julius 128, 133, 134
Harris, Larry 159
Harris, Susan Straughn 87, 88
"Harry & Daphne" 39

"Harry's Houseguest" 66-67
"Hart to Heart" 123
Hawker, John 102
Hawkins, Michael G. 128
Hayes, Gary 122
Hayes, Gloria 128
Haymer, Johnny 127
Haynes, Hilda 39, 43
Haze, Stan 106
Heath, Luise 130
"Heeeere's Johnny" 111, 117
Heffner, Kyle T. 123
Helberg, Sandy 113
Held, Carl 106
Hemsley, Sherman v, 8, 10, 11, 13-14, 24, 26, 30, 34, 36, 37, 45, 46, 52, **74, 75, 76, 81, 82, 85, 86,** 91, 125, 131, 138, 139-140, 141, 142, 143, 147, 148, 149, 152, 157, 158, 160, 161, 165-166, 167, 168
Henderson, Bill 49
Henderson, Maye 28
Henniger, Paul 23
"Henry's Farewell" 10
Herbeck, Bobby 114, 128, 129
Herman, Karen 11, 14, 140
Hester, Ashley 105
Hicks, Maxine Elliott 68
Hightower, Sally 66
Hiller, Stephen A. 90
Hinner, Jackie *see* Roth, Jackie
Hirsch, Lonnie 123
Hoag, Mitzi 96
"Hold Out, The" 68
Holland, Erin and Leslie 105
Hollar, Lloyd 66
Holliday, Kene 106
"Homecoming, Pt. 1, The" 65, 70
"Homecoming, Pt. 2, The" 65, 70
"Honeymoon Hotel" 123-124

Honeymoon Hotel 139
Horn, Alan 163
Horowitz, Andy 129
Houlihan, Keri 131
"House Divided, A" 127
House that George Built, The 103, 107
Houston, Christine 66
"How Not to Marry a Millionaire" 121
"How Now Dow Jones" 112
"How Slowly They Forget" 65, 70-71, **85**
Howard, Bruce 28
Howard, Dennis 89
Hoyos, Teresa V. 111
Huie, Karen 96
Humburger, Larry 114
Humperdinck, Engelbert 128
Hutton, Rif 128

"I Buy the Songs" 97, 100
"I Do, I Don't" 120-121
"I Spy" 104
"I've Got a Secret" 103-104
"I've Still Got It" 103
Iacangelo, Peter 120, 129
Ian, Jonathan 122
"In the Chips" 124
Ingham, Barrie 111, 112
Isaacs, David 39

Jackson, Elma V. 124
Jackson, Jessie 145
Jackson, Leonard 102
Jackson, Mary 130
Jackson, Reggie vi, 129
Jackson, Stoney 129
Jackson, Victoria 104
Jacobs, Jesse 87
Jacobs, Peter 129

Jacobs, Seaman 41, 49, 66, 98, 103
James, Brion 89
Janis, Conrad 49
Jarrell, Andy 106
"Jefferson Airplane" 49
"Jefferson Curve, The" 57, 61-62
"Jefferson vs. Jefferson" 39
"Jeffersons Go to Hawaii, Pt. 1, The" 95, 99
"Jeffersons Go to Hawaii, Pt. 2, The" 95
"Jeffersons Go to Hawaii, Pt. 3, The" 95
"Jeffersons Go to Hawaii, Pt. 4, The" 95-96
"Jeffersons Greatest Hits" 106
Jeffersons Live: The Movin' On Up Tour, The 140
"Jeffersons Move Up, The" 11
Jenious, Crystal 129
"Jenny's Discovery" 48
"Jenny's Grandparents" 39-40
"Jenny's Low" 22, 29
"Jenny's Opportunity" 50
"Jenny's Thesis" 59, 63
Jerald, Penny Johnson 129
Jhones, Pucci 98
Jinaki 56, 60, 61
Joelson, Ben 28
Johnson, Arnold 67
Johnson, Bobby 42
Johnson, Georgann 114
Johnson, Russell 111, 112
"Joltin' George" 88
Jones, Hank 89
Jones, Renee 90
Jordan, Billie 154
Joseph, Bryan 66, 68, 90
Jupiter-Levin, Joey 121

Kaha'ulelio, Damien 95
Kahoano, Kimo 95
Kane, Arnold 28
Kaprall, Bo 28
Karen, James 97
Kaygeyama, Rodney 103
Keahola, Krash 95
Keehne, Virginya 131
Keith, Anita 123
Keith, James 90
Kellermann, Susan 122
Kellogg, Denise 129
Kelly, Calvin 40
Kelton, Kevin 122
Kerr, Judy 127
Kessler, Zale 111
Keyes, Irwin 97, 105, 113, 124
Kiff, Kaleena 96
Kilian, Victor 39
Kilpatrick, Lincoln 95
Kimmel, Joel 41, 127
King, Jr., Martin Luther 15, 24-25, 36, 90-91, 94
King, Kip 128
Kite, Lesa 97
Kline, Wayne 113
Knight, Gladys 114, 116, 117-118
Knight, Jack 66
Koenig, Dennis 50
Kolb, Mina 114
Konrad, Dorothy 111
Kracauer, Hans 114, 130
Kraut, Richard 128
Kravitz, Lenny 16, 147
Kravitz, Sy 15-16
Krebs, Susan 96
Kreinberg, Steve 58
Krinski, Sandy 40
Kubota, Tak 130
Kutras, James 127

La Torre, Tony 128
La Tour, Nick 42, 47
Lacey, Dinah 131
Lacy, Tom 47
Lally, Bob 57, 87, 88, 89, 90, 91, 95, 96, 97, 98, 102, 103, 104, 105, 106, 110, 111, 112, 113, 114, 115, 163
Lampkin, Charles 123, 126
Landers, Judy 68, 72
Larson, Paul 49
LaRusch, Suzanne 127
"Last Dance" 129
"Last Leaf, The" 56
"Laundry is a Tough Town, Pt. 1" 110
"Laundry is a Tough Town, Pt. 2" 110
Lawford, Peter 103, 107
Lawrence, Tom 89
Lawson, Pat 89, 105, 114
Le Vant, Rene 128
Lear, Norman vi, viii, 1-3, 4, 5, 7-8, 9, 10-11, 13, 16, 17, 18, 20, 23, 25, 26, 29, 30, 31, 35, 37, 42, 53-54, 60, 63, 69, 71, **81**, 101, 116, 117, 135, 140, 141, 142, 145, 146, 147, 150, 152, 155, 163, 168
Leavitt, Ron 96, 104, 106, 110, 111, 112, 114, 128, 163
Lebowitz, Neil 87, 89, 111, 121
Lee, David viii, 67, 88, 89, 90, 96, 97, 102, 103, 104, 105, 106, 110, 111, 112, 114, 115, 121, 122, 124, 129, 130, 131, 131, 146-147, 163
Lee, Ruth 39, 43
Leeds, Peter 57
Lehman, Lillian 50, 53
"Lesson in Love" 106

Levant, Brian 49
Levine, Ken 39
Levine, Laura 56
Lew, Joycelyne 103
Libertini, Richard 38
"Lie Detector, The" 47, 52
Lightfoot, Leonard 97, 105
"Like Father, Like Son" 29, 34-35
Lile, Ford 87
Linville, Larry vi, 98
"Lionel Cries Uncle" 28, 33-34
"Lionel Gets the Business" 57
"Lionel Moves In" 9
"Lionel the Playboy" 27
"Lionel's Engagement" 10
"Lionel's Pad" 48
"Lionel's Problem" 41
"List, The" 121
"Loan, The" 90
Long, Avon 9
"Longest Day, The" 90
Lord, Justin 67
Loros, George 89
"Louise Feels Useless" 27, 31
"Louise Forgets" 49
"Louise Gets Her Way" 47, 51-52
"Louise Suspects" 47
"Louise Takes a Stand" 90
"Louise vs. Florence" 88
"Louise vs. Jenny" 49-50
"Louise's Award" 67-68
"Louise's Convention" 68-69
"Louise's Cookbook" 41
"Louise's Daughter" 38
"Louise's Father" 102
"Louise's Friend" 50
"Louise's New Interest" 56
"Louise's Old Boyfriend" 87
"Louise's Painting" 65
"Louise's Physical" 50-51
"Louise's Reunion" 67

"Louise's Setback" 89
"Louise's Sister" 67
Lumbly, Carl 97
"Lunch with Mama" 40
Lussier, Robert 41
Lyles, Tracee 98

Mack, Barnard 68
MacKenzie, Phillip Charles 58, 59
MacMurray, Sam 68
Major, Tony 58
Mann, Howard 122
Manning, Jack 68
Manning, Ruth 57
Manson, Alan 49
"Marathon Men" 95
Marcus, Bill 129
Margolese, E. M. 68
Margulies, Lee 136
Marotta, Albert 87
"Marriage Counselors, The" 50
Marshall, Sarah 98
Marshall, William 111
Martin, Helen 120
Marx, Arthur 39
Mascarino, Pierrinno 130
Mayo, Tobar 58
McCalman, Mason 47
McCay, Peggy 115
McClurg, Edie 111, 112, 130
McCormick, Larry vi, 67
McDonald, William 90
McFrazier, Sean Garrett 96
McGovern, Terrence 127
McGrath, Fred 123
McGrath, George 131
McIntire, James 106
McIntyre, Bill 55
Mckenzie, Richard 47
McNair, Barbara 123, 124
McPhillips, Hugh 98

McVeagh, Eve 89
McWhorter, John H. 165
"Me and Billy Dee" 66, 71-72
"Me and Mr. G" **82**, 89, 92
Meade, Peter ii
Mealy, Barbara 58
"Meet the Press" 28, 34
"Men of the Cloth" 105, 108
Mercer, Ernestine 124
Messina, Lou 112
Meyer, Dorothy 58
Michaels, Margaret 111
Miller, Karen C. 163
Miller, Mark 110
Miller, R. J. 130
Milligan, Mike 38, 40, 41, 48, 49,
   50, 51, 55, 56, 58, 65, 66, 69, 87,
   90, 95, 98, 101, 102, 125, 163
Minchenberg, Richard 90,
Mirliss, Bonnie 115
"Mission Incredible, Pt. 1" 120,
   125
"Mission Incredible, Pt. 2" 120,
   125
"Mission Incredible, Pt. 3" 120,
   125
Mitchell, Gordon "Whitey" ix, 1,
   3, 16, 27, 28, 39, 40, 40, 41, 42,
   47, 48, 49, 50, **84**, 141, 143
Mitchell, Peter 87
Mobley, Candy 66
Monte, Eric 5-6, 53-54
Montgomery, Earl 110
Moody, Lynne 10, 106
Morgan, Donald A. 154
Moriarty, Jay viii-ix, 38, 40, 41,
   48, 49, 50, 51, 55, 56, 58, 65, 66,
   69, 87, 90, 95, 98, 101, 102, 125,
   141, 163
Morrill, Priscilla 57

Morris, Garrett vi, 114, 116, 117, 120, 124, 125
Morris, Greg 120, 125
Moses, David 98
Moss, Winston 127
Mossman, Douglas 96
"Mother Jefferson's Birthday" 41, 43-44, **85**
"Mother Jefferson's Boyfriend" 28, 32
"Mother Jefferson's Fall" 39, 42-43
"Movin' On Down" 39
"Movin' On Up" 25, 32
Moye, Michael G. viii, 88, 89, 91, 95, 97, 98, 103, 105, 110, 111, 114, 120, 123, 125, 128, 131, 146, 147, 163
"Mr. Clean" 114
"Mr. Piano" 27-28, 33
"Mr. Wonderful" 113
Muellerleile, Marianne 112
Murray, Jane 163
Murray, Warren S. 130
Murry, Bill Phillips 88
"My Girl, My Louise" 113
"My Guy, George" 123
"My Hero" 97
"My Maid, My Wife" 113
"My Maid, Your Maid" 102
"My Wife, I Think I'll Keep Her" 105
Myers, Pauline 27

Naff, Lycia 120
Nazarian, Randall 110
Nealy, Frances E. 58, 98
Neigher, Stephen 67, 68, 131
Nevi, Steve 111, 112
"New Girl in Town, A" 123
Newman, Elaine 122
Newman, Pam 129

Nichol, Don 3, 5-6, 8, 23, 26, 27, 38, 39, 40, 143, 163
Nichole, Lydia viii, 105, 148
Nichols, Mike 108
Nicholson, Dave 87
"Night to Remember, A" 90
Nisbet, Lindy 129
Norman, Maidie 39, 43
"Not So Dearly Beloved" 98
"Now You See It, Now You Don't, Pt. 1" 87-88
"Now You See It, Now You Don't, Pt. 2" 88

O'Connor, Carroll 7, 9, 58, **73**, **74**, 140
O'Gilvie, Sylvia 163
O'Leary, John 57
O'Neill, Mary Ellen 96
"Odd Couple, The" 131
"Off-Off-Off-Off Broadway" 131
Ogilvie, Sylvia 163
"Old Flame, The" 50, 53
Oleson, Carole 114
Olfson, Ken 113
Oliver, Deanna 128
"Once a Friend" 55, 60, 146, 162
"Once Upon a Time" 91
"One Flew Into the Cuckoo's Nest" 89
"Ones You Love, The" 68
Orr, David 91
"Other Woman, The" 68, 72
"Otis" 123, 126

Pagliaro, Joanne 88
Palachio, Moki 96
Parker, F. William 56, 90
Pataki, Michael 114
Paul, Georgie 58
Paymer, David 120

Payne, Lee 96
Peluce, Meeno 96
Pendleton, David 55
Penn, Edward 104
"Personal Business" 115
Perzigian, Jerry 68, 69, 87, 88, 89, 90, 97, 102, 103, 104, 106, 111, 113, 114, 115, 122, 123, 129, 130, 163
Petrullo, Joe 66
Phelan, Robert 68
Phillips, Lester 50
Phillips, Ralph 106
Pinkard, Fred 39
Pitt, Brad 145
Plumb, Susan 114
Podell, Rick 105
"Poetic Justice" 112
Pollack, Brian 105
Pollack, Donna Marcione 154
Ponzini, Antony 58
Poryes, Michael 113
Potter, Betsey 144, 154
Potter, Don 87
Premice, Josephine 67
Preston, J. A. 40
Price, Paul B. 97
Prokopuk, Michael 127
"Put It On" 96

Quilan, Eddie 90

Ralph, Sheryl Lee vi, 68
Ramsey, Logan 104
Ramsey, Marion 41
Randolph, Amanda 44
Randolph, Lillian vi, 41, 43-44, **85**
Rasulala, Thalmus 57
Ray, James 68
"Real Men Don't Dry Clean" 122
"Red Robins" 131, 137

Redd, Veronica 55
Reddy, Helen 128, 132, 133
Reed, Albert vi, 28, 33-34
Reiner, Carl 7
Reiner, Rob 7-8, **73**
"Retirement Party" 48
"Return of Bentley, The" 121
Reynolds, Dale 127
Ricard, Adrian 58, 112
"Rich Man's Disease" 28
Rich, John 9
Richman, Jeffrey 105, 113, 120, 127
Riggs, Rita **84**, 144, 155-156
Riley, Andy 95
Ritz, James 39, 41
Rizzi, Ben 38
Roberts, Davis 42, 68
Roberts, Don 164
Robins, Bumper 121
Robinson, Matt 131
Robinson, Roger 88
Rodine, Alex 104
Rodrigues, Percy 56
Rogers III, Lou 98
Rogers, Jim 58, 59, 66
Roker, Roxie 11, 14-16, 24, 26, 31, 36, 46, 70, 72, **74, 76, 77, 80, 93**, 116, 131, 132, 136, 139, 140, 142, 143-144, 147, 167
Rolike, Hank 56, 60, 61
Rolle, Esther **84**, 154, 167, 169
Rosario, Joe 105, 128
Rose, Robin Pearson 120
Rosemond, Don 154
Rosen, Sy 163
Rosenberg, Arthur 90
Ross, Gene 127
Ross, Mickey 3, 4-6, 8, 23, 26, 27, 38, 39, 40, **84**, 163
Ross, Stefan 114

Ross, Ted vi, 65, 70, 71, **85**
Roth, Jackie 131
Rothman, Mark viii, 104, 107-108
Rubenstein, Phil 103, 131
Rubin, Andrew 29, 141 149-150
Rudolph, Stu 156
Ruttan, Susan vi, 130

Sampson, Robert 48
Sanders, Henry G. 50
Sandford, Richard 95
Sands, Billy 49, 110
Sanford and Son 19, 22, 32, 53, 145, 155, 169
Sanford, Isabel v, 8, 9, 11, 12-13, 23, 26, 29, 30, 31, 36, 37, 69, **74, 75, 76, 81, 82, 85, 86**, 101, 109, 116-117, 124, 131, 137, 138, 139-140, 147, 149, 157, 158, 159, 160, 161, 165, 166, 167, 168
Saunders, J. Jay 49
Savant, Joseph 129
"Sayonara, Pt. 1" 129, 134-135
"Sayonara, Pt. 2" 129, 134-135
Scannell, Kevin 89
Schiller, Bob **84**
Schilling, William G. 122
Schrum, Peter 106, 114, 118, 119
Schwartz, Gary 87
Scorpio, Jay 121
Scott, Fred D. 88
Scott, Larry B. 129
Scott, Oz 120, 121, 122, 123, 127, 128, 129, 130, 131
Scott, Susie 129
Scott, Timothy 123
"Secret in the Back Room, A" 130
Seeger, Sara 65
Segall, Don 56
Segall, Pamela *see* Adlon, Pamela
Segall, Penina 131

Seigel, Donald L. 68, 69, 87, 88, 89, 90, 97, 102, 103, 104, 106, 111, 113, 114, 115, 122, 123, 129, 130, 163
Selzer, Milton 27
"Separation, Pt. 1, The" 102
"Separation, Pt. 2, The" 102
Seymour, Jeff 91
Shamshak, Sam 96
Shannon, Maureen 89
Sharkey, Ray 42
Sharpe, S. Pearl 50
Shaw, Rick 105
Shea, Jack 27, 28, 29, 38, 39, 40, 41, 42, 47, 48, 49, 50, 55, 56, 57, 58, 59, 65, 66, 67, 68, 69, 163
Shea, Patt 55, 58
Sheiner, Mary-David 87
Shelley, Dave 58, 130
Shelton, Reid 129
Shepard, Richard 87
Shephard, Harvey 132
"Short Story, A" 87
"Shower, The" 89-90
Shulman, Roger 27, 55, 56, 57, 58, 62, 160
Sienna, Bridget 131
Silva, Tim 130
"Silver Lining" 115
Silverman, David 96, 97, 98
Singletary, Tony 122, 153, 156, 163
Sister Sledge vi, 123, 124
"Small Fish, Big Pond" 98
"Small Victory, A" 106
Smith, Arlando 124, 128, 153, 154, 163
Smith, Dwan 57
Smith, Ebonie 22, 127, 129, 131, 134
"Social Insecurity" 111

Somack, Jack 57
"Some Enchanted Evening" 128
Sommerfield, Diane 38
"Sorry, Wrong Meeting" 97
Sparks, Don 97
Spears, Vida 131
Spevack, Melodee 114
Spinks, Michael 128, 132, 133
Sprung, Sandy 113, 115, 122, 128
Staley, James 55
Stanley, Alvin 88
Stanley, Diane Messina 112
Stanley, Rebecca 113
Stapleton, Jean 7, 11, 58, **73**, 141
Starks, Roger 97
"State of Mind" 130
Steinkellner, Bill 127, 129, 130, 131
Steinkellner, Cheri *see* Eichen, Cheri
Stellone, Al 87
Stern, Elliot 110
Stevens, Brent 113
Stevens, Dorit 97
Stevens, Wade 113
Stevenson, Billy 88
Stevenson, Rosalind 122
Stewart, Lynne Marie 115
Stewart, Milton "Mel" 8-9, 10
Stoiber, Edmund 67
Stone, Rob 115
Stratton, Jan 113
"Strays, Pt. 1, The" 105
"Strays, Pt. 2, The" 105, 148
Strickland, Amzie 113
Struthers, Sally 8, 11, **73**
Stump, Ken 163
Stuthman, Fred 56
Sullivan, J. Christopher 96
Sun, Young 111
Sunga, George 163

Susskind, Steve 129
Sustarsic, Stephen 96, 97, 98
Sutherland, Esther 89, 105, 114
Sutton, Henry 87
Sutton, Neal 88
Swarbrick, Carol 66
"Sweet Georgia Brown" 152
Swertlow, Frank S. 30

Talbott, Michael 123
Talisman, David 47
Tari, La 58
Tarloff, Eric 28, 39
Tarloff, Frank 29, 38
Tasco, Rai 120
Ta-Tanisha 89
Taylor, Kurt 48, 67, 110, 123
Taylor, Myra 89, 105
"Tennis, Anyone?" 42
Tepper, Herbie 87
"Thammy the Thongwriter" 104
"That Blasted Cunningham" 130
"They Don't Make Preachers Like Him Anymore" 128, 133-134
"Thomas H. Willis & Co" 58
Thomas, Ernest L. vi, viii, 39, 44, 148-149
Thomas, M. Martez 67
Thompkins, Anthony 59
"Three Faces of Florence" 68
Till Death Us Do Part 2-3
Tobin, Mathew 57
Tolbert, Berlinda viii, 10, 11, 18-19, 24, 26, 29, 36, 46, 52, **74**, **76**, 102, 110, 114-115, 116, 129, 130, 142-145, 155, 167
"Tom the Hero" 48
Torres, Liz vi, 98
Tracy, Steve 106
"Trading Places" 122-123
Trice, Ron 58, 59

"True Confessions" 114, 117
"Truth Hurts, The" 131
"Try a Little Tenderness" 128
Tuell, John 89
Turgeon, Peter 68
Turner, Dain 114
Turner, Lloyd 3, 4, 27, 28, 39, 40, 41, 42, 47, 48, 49, 50
Tyler, Ginny 48
Tyler, Willie and Lester viii, 66, 71, **81**, 150-152
Tyner, Charles 123

"Uncle Bertram" 39
"Uncle George and Aunt Louise" 58
Unger, Arthur 35
"Unnatural, The" 129
Usen, Skip 66

Vallance, Olga 56
Veith, Sandy 42
Vigran, Herb 130
Vince, Nancy 57, 65, 102
"Visitors, The" 56, 60-61
Voland, Herb 57
Vosburgh, Marcy 113, 115, 122, 128

Wade, Adam 68
Wai, Clay 95, 96
Wainwright, Ernie 67
Waldron, Bhetty 56, 59
Walker, Charles 87, 88
Ward, Kate 114
Ward, Richard 48
Warfield, Marlene 89
Washington, Erwin 65
Washington, Vernon 55, 57, 66, 68, 88
Watson, James A. 66, 106

Watson, Vernee 103
"We Are the World" 133
Weaver, Les 49
Webster, Diana 102
Weddell, Vernon 89
"Wedding, The" 42
Weinstein, Sol 47, 57, 67
Weisberg, Sheila Judis 87
Weiskopf, Kim 55, 60, 121, 146, 162
Weiskoph, Bob **84**
Wells, Aarika 121
Wells, Danny 22, 26, 29, 38, 55, 65, 66, 87, 88, 90, 97, 98, 103, 105, 106, 121, 128, 129, 130, 131, 135, 141
Wendel, Elmarie 130
Wertimer, Ned 11, 21-22, 26, 28, 38, 39, 40, 41, 42, 47, 48, 49, 55, 56, 57, 58, 59, 66, 67, 69, **74**, 90, 91, 96, 108
Wesley, John 121
West, Bernie 3, 4-5, 6, 8, 23, 26, 27, 38, 39, 40, 163
Weston, Jim 97
"What Are Friends For?" 66
"What Makes Sammy Run" 122, 125-126
What's Happening 44, 54
"Wheel of Forever, The" 115
Wheeler, Margaret 65
"Where's Papa?" 88
White, Al 57, 121
White, Jaleel 127, 162
White, Myrna 98, 123
White, Peter 112
"Who's the Fairest?" 121
"Whole Lot of Trouble, A" 103
Wilhoite, Kathleen 130
Williams, Billy Dee vi, 66, 71-72, 99, 128, 161

Williams, Dick Anthony 89
Williams, Hal 50, 128
Williams, Jr., Larry O. 122
Williams, Randy 58
Williams, Rene 155
Williams, Tom 98
Willie, Dap "Sugar" 114
Willis, Penelope 89
Wills (DeWindt), Sheila 112
Wilson, Ailene **82**, 89
Wilson, Grant 120
Wilson, Norman D. 114, 118
Wilson, Teddy 57
Wilton, Garth 122
Wise, Alfie 58
Wisehart, Bob 70
Witt, Mike 129
Wittington, Dick 68
Wolterstorff, Robert 48, 50, 57, 59, 65, 67, 68, 88, 89

Woodard, Bill 58
Woods, Renn viii, 123, 150
Workman, C. Lindsay 51
Worsham, Doris 143
Wright, Wendell 91
Wyle, Michael 128

Yama, Michael 128
Yammy, Dick 129
Yorkin, Bud 2-3, 7-8
"You'll Never Get Rich" 128, 133
Young, Anna 121
Young, Keone 111
Young, Stephen 48, 50
Young, William Allen 96
Youngfellow, Barrie 67

Zadikov, Greg 106
Zakarin, Mark 130

www.ingramcontent.com/pod-product-compliance
Lightning Source LLC
Chambersburg PA
CBHW051927160426
43198CB00012B/2072